ANALYSIS OF COLLECTIVE BARGAINING ON CONTINUING VOCATIONAL TRAINING IN FRANCE

T0162916

ANALYSIS OF COLLECTIVE BARGAINING ON CONTINUING VOCATIONAL TRAINING IN FRANCE

by

JACQUES ROJOT

Université de Paris-I, Panthéon-Sorbonne

and

JEAN-MARIE LUTTRINGER

Université de Paris-X, Nanterre

1995

This report was written in collaboration with J. -L. Ferrand (CNAM) and P. Guilloux (IUT de Vannes). The field surveys were conducted by M. Blin, H. Fine, V. Michelet and L. Pham.

ISBN 90-6831-661-3
D. 1995/0602/9

TABLE OF CONTENTS

GENERAL INTRODUCTION

A. *Goals of the report*

In close co-operation with the organizations representing the social partners at Community level, the European Community is supporting the development of a standardized analysis of collective agreements and company-level agreements on continuing vocational training in each of the Member States. It is fostering the exchange of experience between employers' and employees' organizations and joint bodies in order to stimulate the spread of innovatory contractual agreements.

The present report constitutes the French contribution to this initiative. It is aimed at responding to the three goals which were set for the rapporteurs: to provide a snapshot of the present situation regarding collective bargaining on vocational training in France; to single out discernible innovations; and to present the findings in a form which will help to promote the exchange of experience between social partners in different Member States. It is, therefore, "operational" rather than "theoretical" in its emphasis.

Although the common methodological framework suggested to the rapporteurs of all twelve Member States has been used as a basic guide, it has been adapted to the French situation, which is particularly comprehensive in this field in comparison with other European countries.

B. *The French context*

Since 1970, collective bargaining has been one of the determining factors in the development of continuing training in France, alongside action by the legislators and the public authorities: the text constituting the cornerstone of the French system of continuing training is a national multi-industry agreement of that year, supplemented by numerous amendments, renewed on 3 July 1991 and extended and disseminated by the law.

The 1970/1991 multi-industry agreement represents the source of an individual right to training, a network of joint institutions for the administration of training and "programmatic" provisions outside any statutory requirements.

The legislative reforms on collective bargaining introduced in 1982 (Auroux law) and 1984 (Rigout law) stimulated collective bargaining at enterprise level and sector level. In addition to distinguishing three separate bargaining levels (national multi-industry, sector, enterprise), they expanded the scope of bargaining and specified bargaining on particular issues at each particular level: creation of joint institutions, right to and priority of access to training for individuals, financing, the linking of employment and training, training and the acquisition of skills, combined training-and-work and other training formulas, certification, etc.

Such bargaining issues are all the more important inasmuch as they have bearing not only on desirable directions of development but also on methods of resolving problems and legal rules, and involve substantial financial resources.

Without doubt, therefore, the two decades of French practice in collective bargaining as applied to continuing training offer an abundant source of material for consideration at Community level. The very magnitude of the task meant, however, that in the case of France the research goals and methods needed to be defined with great care.

C. Methodological choices

1. Owing to the wealth and diversity of the relevant material, the French rapporteurs opted to concentrate on Part II of the outline suggested to the national teams, namely, on the analysis of contractual policy. Other studies and reports are already available on the matters mentioned in the outline's General Introduction and Part I (information on the labour market, the education and training systems and the industrial relations system). Similarly, since there is a system in France for processing statistics on vocational training (Finance Law, CEREQ) the rapporteurs did not make any specific inquiries on this point among the enterprises questioned. All such elements not included in the core of the French report have been made available in the form of notes and working documents to the European rapporteur responsible for the General Report.

2. The rapporteurs did, however, think it useful to include a brief description of the French system of initial and continuing vocational training (Part I), as being necessary to a proper understanding of the procedures and issues of collective bargaining in this field.

3. The surveys covered eight sectors, with two enterprises in each sector. The sectors were those suggested to all the national rapporteurs by the initial outline (construction, textiles, metals, banking, insurance, retail distribution and hotels and catering), to which we added the chemical industry.

It was not always possible to select sample enterprises from among small or even medium-sized ones: in certain sectors (e.g. banking) there are simply no small enterprises at all, and in other instances no small or medium-sized enterprise engaged in the training activity relevant to the subject of the report could be identified. The sample enterprises used were identified through relevant actors in each of the sectors.

4. The methodology used was strictly that of field work. Initial access to the actors was provided at the outset through the secretariats of the National Joint Committees on Employment (CPNEs). In each sector, discussions were held with the signatories of collective agreements and/or members of the CPNEs. These discussions were supplemented by analysis of available documents.

A similar model was adopted for the individual enterprises whenever this was possible and applicable (agreement, dialogue, etc.). Informal bargaining arrangements and the role of the works council were taken into account.

It should be noted that, since employers in France are obliged by law to finance continuing vocational training in the form of a contribution representing a specified percentage of the wage bill, statistics on the recipients of training, its duration, types, etc. have to conform to the fiscal requirements in accordance with which they are declared annually, and were not available in the form suggested to the national rapporteurs. It was therefore not possible to present enterprise statistical tables in the form specified.

5. It should be noted that the sector and enterprise case-studies which are annexed to the report were systematically authenticated with the actors encountered, who are therefore recognizable in the "snapshot" presented by the research team.

D. *Structure*

The structure adopted for the report is the outcome of the above considerations and comprises three main sections, in addition to this Introduction and the General Conclusions:

Part I: Characteristics of the French system of initial and continuing vocational training

Part II: Contractual policy on continuing vocational training: legal framework and main results

Part III: Contractual policy on continuing vocational training in eight sectors

PART I: CHARACTERISTICS OF THE FRENCH SYSTEM OF INITIAL AND CONTINUING VOCATIONAL TRAINING

A. Introductory Remarks

In comparison with other countries, notably in Europe, France has an education system made singular by a number of features which, although not necessarily specific, are particularly strongly and sharply defined and embody significant characteristic dichotomies.

Firstly, the distinction between education and initial training on the one hand and continuing training on the other, which in concrete terms have developed in line with differing chronological influences and differing objectives. Most French educational institutions have their origin in the distant past and appear to have accumulated one on top of another as if by a process of sedimentation; hence, many structures of education and initial training (universities, lycées, the comprehensive schools called collèges, grandes écoles, vocational education, primary schooling) are creations of or tolerated inheritances from the *ancien régime* which have been modernized or simply adapted to the conventions of modern-day France and have never really broached the question of continuing training, except in the second half of the twentieth century. It is only in perhaps the last ten years or so that this question, so important in the context of the construction of Europe, has actually been tackled in France.

Secondly, the opposition between the role of central government and that of other economic actors. Education and initial training in particular, but also continuing training to a lesser extent, are stamped by the founding, financing and controlling role of the French State, which has always created their structures, laid down their rules and dictated their programmes according to its own logic through the Ministry of National Education and a monopoly of the award of degrees and diplomas. Nowadays, the preponderance of the State is starting to be called into question, at least in terms of discussion and intentions, but for all practical purposes it remains quite fundamental.

As both a cause and a consequence of this dimension, there is also the traditional and secular opposition between public and private, the latter corresponding to the denominational education which was predominant under the *ancien régime*. After 1789, the republican and hence lay French State fought against the influence of private denominational education, which was suspected of sympathizing with a return of the monarchists, throughout the nineteenth century. Nowadays, freedom of education is guaranteed by the Constitution and private education is linked contractually with the public authorities, but it is nevertheless still subject to the dictates of the latter and the strong public protests of 1984 demonstrated that the old antagonism was still alive, and indeed alive in the minds of many citizens.

Another consequence of the strength of the state and its national peculiarities, the centralism of administration in France, has entailed the centralism of education and what has nowadays become the highly topical opposition between the national level on the one hand and the regional or local level on the other. For decades, the quasi-monopoly of the Ministry of National Education meant that the education system was steered centrally, although the local authorities were from a very early stage involved in elementary education. However, the political and administrative centralism in the matter of education (as also in other public spheres) that was long characteristic of the French system has been overturned since the laws on decentralization were passed: decentralization of continuing vocational training in 1984 and decentralization of education and initial training in 1984 and 1985, each using differing ways and means. Today, the system has not stabilized and the problem of the effective distribution of powers and influence between national level and local (region, département and commune) level represents one of the key questions of educational planning during these closing years of the century in France.

Lastly, there is the other notable opposition in the French system between general education and technical and vocational education. The latter has been very largely underestimated and even devalued both quantitatively and qualitatively, particularly as regards initial training, in favour of a more universalist view of professional abilities (apart from the subsystem of the Grandes Ecoles, another typically French feature). This opposition is, in point of fact, founded in a more weighty social phenomenon, namely, the gulf separating the world of education from the world of economic activity and production, with each knowing nothing of the other. Here too, it is only in recent years that these two closed worlds have begun to collaborate, and this erosion of the division between them is one of the cardinal issues of the present decade. The role of the social partners, as being present in both systems, can in the future only increase.

B. Chapter I. Education and initial training

§1. General structure of the system

The general structure of the French system of education and initial training may be represented diagrammatically as shown in Annex 1.

Its logic prompts the following comments:

(a) The importance of general education: the system includes little specialization, but is intended to develop in the individual a high level of general knowledge, culture, and abilities which are transferable to many occupational sectors. Historically, the courses taught long remained predominantly theoretical, with priority for subjects of a scientific and, later, technical nature but little for those of a more directly vocational kind. The baccalauréat certificate itself, the key element of the system, remained predominantly generalist up till the 1970s and has only very recently been genuinely diversified.

(b) The system functions as a "funnel-shaped" continuum from nursery school (pre-primary schooling) to university: starting from a very broad base aiming to give the same basic education to all citizens (republican ideal), it narrows progressively until it ends in the grandes écoles and the universities, the latter being seen from the outset as the culmination of the entire system for everybody. This is why it is frequently described as an élitist system which generates failure, since most of those who leave the system do so because of inability to pursue the "royal road" leading to the baccalauréat and university.

(c) There is little flexibility as regards pupils, rates of learning and development, particularly in primary and secondary education. Each class is deemed to be appropriate to a standard age and a progressive degree of difficulty which do not necessarily correspond to the reality of the cognitive structures and social and emotional problems of young people; the result is yet more failure, early drop-outs from the system and the existence for the last thirty years of special or remedial classes, parallel courses for children with particular learning difficulties (special schooling) and the adjustment of courses.

(d) Technical and vocational education became established in the system at a late stage, "grafted" on to it, as it were, and in reality catering for pupils who fail in the lengthy and noble pursuit of the baccalauréat; this gives it an often negative image in public opinion and influences the choices made by parents for their childrens' education, and the consequence is the difficulties sometimes encountered by employers in hiring appropriately skilled staff.

§2. Quantitative data: pupil and student numbers, and institutions

In 1990, the French education system accommodated 13.7 million pupils and students, distributed as shown in Annex 2. Thus, one person in every four of the French population, counting all age groups together, is present in the education system as a recipient, and this is even with the following categories excluded:

(a) the 228,000 apprentices in Apprentice Training Centres (CFAs);
(b) the 210,000 primary and secondary pupils who come under ministries other than the Ministry of National Education (particularly the Ministry of Agriculture);
(c) all individuals, of whatever age, receiving forms of adult vocational training.

The importance of the education system in French society is, therefore, considerable and is continuing to increase, not only in absolute numbers but also relative to the parallel growth in the population: between 1960 and 1990 the number of pupils and students rose by almost 40% whereas the total population increased by only just over 20%. This trend is the combined result of the entry into education of age groups from the "baby boom" of the 1950s, a relative democratization of education, and the economic necessity of improving the level of training of young people emerging from the education system, which has automatically extended the overall length of their education.

This phenomenon, which is common to the post-war Western economies, is thrown into particularly sharp relief in France by the monolithic and in some respects élitist nature of the system as described earlier, which is designed to "narrow" as the level ascends, whereas the reality of the system is very different: although primary education represents a basis which is more or less stable over time (pupil numbers of 5-7 million), this is not the case with either secondary education (collèges and lycées) or higher education, which have witnessed a considerable swelling in their numbers for the past twenty years: from 4 million to close on 6 million pupils for lycées and collèges, and from 0.5 to 1.5 million students for higher education.

This growth trend, which has occurred rapidly and is to some degree contradictory to the logic of the way in which the system functions, is the reason why over the past two decades successive Ministers for National Education have applied or attempted to apply reforms of different kinds to secondary and higher education, with uneven success: the Edgard Fauré Law of 1968 on higher education, and the Haby reforms of 1975 and Legrand reforms of 1982 on secondary collèges and lycées. Among other things, these reforms have three main objectives:

(1) to provide better adaptation to population trends, make more appropriate provision for the specific characteristics of pupils and students, and develop innovations in teaching;
(2) to strengthen and develop the provision of technical and vocational education and training, apart from apprenticeship, in secondary and higher education;
(3) to open up the world of education to its social and occupational environment so that it can better meet the needs of the economic world and improve young people's chances of finding a job corresponding to the level of skill qualification they have attained.

These reforms are, nevertheless, proving slow to be implemented and, in particular, have not fundamentally called into question the relative isolation of the education system (which is steered totally by the Ministry of National Education) from the world of production.

Lastly, it should be noted that, of the whole of primary and secondary education, the state education system represents 83% of establishments and 86% of pupils, with private education under government contract accounting for 17% and 14% respectively.

§3. Nomenclature of levels of education and training

A nomenclature of the levels of education and training and their theoretical correspondence with levels of skill qualification and employment has been in force since 1969. It is divided into six categories, as follows:

Education/Training	Level	Qualification/skill level
End of compulsory schooling (age 16)	VI	Unskilled worker
Short training (1 year at most) Vocational Education Certificate (CEP). Often no training	Vb	Semi-skilled worker
Vocational Studies Certificate (BEP) Certificate of Vocational Competence (CAP)	V	Skilled worker or White-collar worker
Baccalauréat Technician Certificate Vocational Certificate or Supervisor Certificate Vocational baccalauréat	IV	Technician or Supervisor
Advanced Technician Certificate (BTS) University Diploma in Technology (DUT) First two-year stage at university: General University Diploma (DEUG)	III	Senior Technician
Grandes Ecoles, Ecoles d'Ingénieurs and Universities (stages 2 and 3)	I and II	Graduate engineer Senior Professional and Managerial Staff

The employment grades corresponding to these various levels are defined in Annex 3.

This nomenclature reveals the pyramidal structure of the education system, and in particular the fact that vocational education is confined to the lower levels; but it also reflects a Taylorian division of labour within the production apparatus which has long been predominant in French enterprises and which explains why this nomenclature has served as a basis for collective agreements signed between social partners.

Nevertheless, for 10-15 years the progressive de-Taylorization of production methods in enterprises has been tending to make this typology inappropriate and has prompted the social partners to negotiate job classification scales which accommodate the types of training specific to each sector and correspond more closely to the actual trend in jobs and tasks. The national agreement on job classifications which was signed in 1975 in the metals sector constituted an innovation in this area and has led the way for subsequent similar agreements in other sectors. However, this problem of effective correspondence between education/training levels and skill levels remains a major stake in the education system for the coming years and a central issue of bargaining between employers' and employee's representatives.

§4. Distribution of the numbers leaving the education system

The figures for departures from the system in 1990 were:

34,300	at	level VI
64,000	at	levelVb
291,300	at	level V
140,600	at	level IV
95,800	at	level III
115,400	at	levels II and I.

In other words, a total of 741,400 with 39.3% of departures occuring at level V alone. This prompts several comments.

First, the fact that the entire system is having difficulty in keeping up with the rapid rise in skill levels in enterprises: 53% of young people are emerging from the education system with a level V or below, whereas employers increasingly require level IV and above for highly skilled manual and white-collar jobs and technicians. At present, the shortfall is being made up by means of internal policies on continuing vocational training for employees. The gap also explains why the Ministry of National Education has set itself the target of 80% for departures at baccalauréat age (level IV) by the year 2000.

Second, it can be seen that close on 100,000 young people emerge from education and initial training with a level VI or Vb, *i.e.* without any real vocational qualifications. This flow has been more or less constant for some twenty years and nowadays constitutes the source of the mass of first-time job-seekers who fail to gain entry to the labour market and for whom over the past ten years or so the French Government, like all other European Governments, has been introducing various policies, plans and measures aimed at absorbing them into employment. The genuine (even if limited) effectiveness of such action is not, however, enough to check the problem at source, since a new crop of these unqualified young people joins the economically active population every year. The social partners have tackled the problem, and in the national multi-industry agreement of 25 October 1983 instituted a series of measures on special contracts of employment incorporating combined training-and-work, thereby involving employers. The Government, in its turn, continued to finance this form of "extended initial vocational training" substantially by exempting participating employers from payment of social security contributions. From the legal standpoint, all such measures are nowadays fully integrated in the vocational training system and therefore entirely within the field of competence of the social partners.

§5. Technical and vocational education

Despite the fact that it encompasses the majority of pupil and student numbers and departures from initial training in the education system, this strand, grafted onto the existing strands of general education, has always had difficulty in finding a true identity of its own and avoiding being seen as the route of failure for those unable to continue as far as the baccalauréat in its capacity as the normal culmination of successful studies.

As a result, technical and vocational education is dominated by level V qualifications, as shown by the following breakdown of formal qualifications for 1990:

CAP	(Certificate of Vocational Competence):	273,933
BEP	(Vocational Studies Certificate):	162,553
BP	(Vocational Certificate):	13,367
BT	(Technician Certificate):	8,932
Technical baccalauréat:		113,993
Vocational baccalauréat:		33,124
BTS	(Advanced Technician Certificate):	52,833
DUT	(University Diploma in Technology):	27,835
Graduate Engineer Diploma:		16,080

Thus, the level V certificates CAP and BEP represent, on their own, 62% of the total of 701,810 and the majority of departures from the education system. This means that technical and vocational education has difficulty in functioning as a separate strand displaying a continuum in terms of flows of numbers, even though in terms of courses it is theoretically possible for a student to progress from the CAP to the Graduate Engineer Diploma. This structuring of the levels of formal qualifications and hence (in theory) skills poses a problem for sectoral representatives and employers, given that the needs of the economy and the production system are pushing up the level significantly and rapidly as a result of the introduction of new technologies, industrial reorganization and new management methods. This is why the education authorities have launched numerous successive reforms in an attempt to adapt education and training to the world of work:

(a) Creation of IUTs (University Institutes of Technology) in 1966 offering, for the first time, two-year or three-year courses leading to post-baccalauréat qualifications (DUT and BTS).

(b) Progressive institution since the 1970s of technical baccalauréats with specialized options (industrial, commercial, etc) and then in 1986 vocational baccalauréats, which are not yet fully developed.

(c) Revision of the certificates for technical education, particularly the CAP and BEP, which are largely based on a traditional "craft" or occupation concept which in many sectors is beginning to be thrown into question by changes in circumstances and the nature of the work.

(d) Reforms of the collèges and lycées; there is no doubt that today these still constitute the core of the problem, and in any case affect the great majority of pupils and students in this strand; personalized education programmes, establishment projects and an opening-up to the environment and the world of work are all in progress.

(e) Administrative decentralization of initial training in 1984, transferring the construction and staffing of collèges to the départements and that of lycées to the regions, with overall control of teaching remaining in the hands of the Ministry of National Education. In practice, however, as a result of development of the educational map at regional level and the fact that the sectoral organizations often enjoy preferential relations with the regional councils, the world of work is beginning to establish closer contacts with technical education.

(f) Introduction in 1989 of new routes of training for engineers via continuing training and apprenticeship. There are too few engineers in France, particularly in comparison with other European countries: it is estimated that the number of engineers emerging annually from the system needs to be doubled. These new (known as "Decomps") training routes are an innovation in the French system in that they signal a blurring of the separation between initial training and continuing training. Large enterprises and the occupational associations are strongly motivated towards their introduction.

(g) The most recent innovations include the creation of IUPs (Vocational University Institutes), with a student intake from the baccalauréat level plus one, created within the universities and leading in three years to a master's degree for engineers in fields outside the traditional engineering disciplines (management, finance, etc.). More recently still, the CNEP (National Commission for Vocational Education) was created.

§6. Apprenticeship system

1. Historical background and manner of functioning

Historically and quantitaively, apprenticeship is a special phenomenon in the French education system. The Astier law of 1919, supplemented by the Finance Law of 1925 on the creation of the apprenticeship tax, laid the foundations for this form of vocational education, almost non-existent at the time, as an element of initial training.

Its purpose is to implement a form of technical and vocational training very closely linked to the world of work in terms of both structure and teaching, with the effective involvement of employers and occupational associations. This has meant its marginalization in relation to the general philosophy of education and initial training, dominated by lengthy and generalist courses culminating in the baccalauréat.

The manner in which the system functions is original: it involves a combination of different actors.

(a) a young person (the apprentice) who enters into an apprenticeship contract with an employer: this is a special contract of employment including a large training element;

(b) an employer who hires the young person and undertakes to ensure that they receive the training specified by the contract in a recognized training centre but also to provide training in the work situation by appointing an apprenticeship master for the purpose;

(c) a vocational training centre: originally an apprenticeship centre, nowadays an Apprentice Training Centre (CFA). Most of these CFAs are managed or controlled by the corresponding occupational associations;

(d) central government, which authorizes forms of training and apprenticeship masters, awards diplomas, controls teaching and contributes to financing through equipment and operating subsidies.

From the start, the teaching principle on which the system is based has been a combination of on-the-job training at the place of work and theoretical instruction at a training centre, a principle which is nowadays claimed by most forms of education and training but which is very difficult to implement in practice.

Financing is provided through an apprenticeship tax levied on all employers, nowadays equal to 0.6% of the gross wage bill, plus subsidies from central government and regional councils.

2. The new context of the 1980s

In the French education system, apprenticeship has always been in a position of marginalization, or even inferiority, in comparison with other forms of initial training. It has often served as the overflow or fall-back solution for pupils who have failed academically in more "high-flown" courses. Hence its frequently negative image in the view of parents, which is very difficult to dispel nowadays; hence its limited extent in numerical terms (for fifty years the number of apprentices in France has been about 200,000); and hence, also, the wish of the public authorities and the occupational associations to change this state of affairs. Two new and influential pieces of legislation have moved in this direction: the Law of 1983 on decentralization and the Law of 1987 on the redefinition of the apprenticeship system.

The Law of 7 January 1983 on the transfer of powers from central government to local authorities conferred on the regional councils responsibility under general law for continuing vocational training and apprenticeship. The apprenticeship system is therefore now under the responsibility of locally elected bodies, closer to the effective field of action of the employers and sectoral organizations (which enjoy preferential relations with the regional councils) and, as it were, "singled out" from initial training to constitute a separate form of training.

The reforming Law of 23 July 1987 substantially expands the requirements and scope of apprenticeship, with the intention of turning it into a complete system of technical training in its own right:

– by increasing the length of training in Apprentice Training Centres and the powers and responsibilities of apprenticeship masters;
– by raising the upper age limit (25);
– and, above all, by raising the level of technical and vocational training to which it can lead: the BTS (Advanced Technician Certificate) and Graduate Engineer Diploma, *i.e.* the highest levels of technical qualification, are now accessible from apprenticeship status.

In theory, therefore, these two laws create a set of conditions which make it possible for apprenticeship to constitute a separate and complete education system in technical and vocational subjects midway between initial training and continuing vocational training, to shake off its negative image of failure and low levels of qualification, and to become comparable with systems in other countries, particularly in Europe. The reality is, however, still very different from this.

3. Structure of the apprentice group

Overall, in spite of the legislative and financial measures aimed at promoting the system the number of apprentices and apprenticeship contracts signed has remained stable for decades, covering around 200,000 young people:

1979:	207,613
1982:	228,726
1985:	213,480
1987:	232,425

The latest figures known, for 1989-90, indicate 231,572 apprentices excluding the agriculture sector (for which the figure is 10,673 for the same period).

The number of contracts signed (intake into the system) shows a very slight downward trend:

130,576	in	1987
132,589	in	1988
137,548	in	1989
129,310	in	1990

The system is predominately male, with girls representing only 29% of the total number; this is mainly due to the nature of the occupations to which it leads. The age pyramid is as follows:

1.1%	of apprentices aged 15
27.2%	of apprentices aged 16
35.7%	of apprentices aged 17
20.1%	of apprentices aged 18
7.9%	of apprentices aged 19
6.8%	of apprentices aged 20
1.2%	of apprentices aged over 20

The structure of the formal qualifications for which apprentices are trained is still very much dominated by level V (leading to skilled manual and white-collar jobs):

level V (CAP)	93.9%
level V (BEP)	1.7%
level IV (BP- Supervisor Certificate)	2.9%
level IV (Vocational baccalauréat)	1.2%
level III (BTS)	0.3%

The agricultural apprenticeship system exhibits the same feature, but with a proportionately higher overall level: only 75% of level V qualifications of the CAP type.

The overwhelming majority of enterprises which employ apprentices are small structures: 80% of apprentices are in enterprises with fewer than 10 employees, 15% in enterprises with 10-50 employees and only 5% in enterprises with over 50 employees. The new Law has brought about a tendency for some large enterprises to hire apprentices, but this is primarily for levels IV and III and is still extremely marginal to the system as a whole.

This pattern is due to the dominance of the sectors which make use of apprenticeship: the forms of training being given to apprentices in 1986 fall into the following groups:

27.5%	for food-related occupations
17%	for construction sector occupations
14.7%	for the health and personal services sector
12.3%	for the retail and distribution sector
11.4%	for the mechanical engineering sector
4.7%	for the forging sector.

All these branches of activity are known to be largely composed of small production units.

4. Apprentice Training Centres and their financing

For the academic year 1989-90, the total number of Apprentice Training Centres (CFAs) for all sectors combined was 633, of which 115 were agricultural. Depending on the legal status and method of administration of CFAs they may come under various supervisory bodies; excluding the agricultural sector, their distribution is as follows:

- 56 CFAs are run by local authorities and their intake represents 6% of all apprentices
- 38 CFAs are run by Chambers of Commerce and Industry for 8% of apprentices
- 61 CFAs are run by public educational establishments for 8% of apprentices
- 73 CFAs are run by trade chambers for 36% of apprentices
- 278 CFAs are run by private bodies for 41% of apprentices
- 12 CFAs are subject to national agreement (1% of apprentices).

In the case of agriculture, 93 CFAs (81%) are attached to public-law bodies and 22 (19%) to private-law bodies.

This distribution shows that CFAs vary widely in size and manner of operation, mainly according to the number and nature of the occupations for which apprentices are prepared. In addition, it should be noted that some are associated with a single industry (for example, building and public works) while others (particularly those run by local authorities) cover a range of different industries.

CFAs do not possess legal personality of their own but have the legal status of agencies; they are regarded as teaching establishments, created by agreement with the public authority. Under this same agreement they have a director and a board allowing them autonomous operation and organization, mainly by means of a specific teaching staff.

Overall, in 1989 the financing of CFAs was apportioned as follows:

Regions	
operating costs	1,497 million francs
equipment	248 million francs
TOTAL	1,745 million francs
Central government	
operating costs	207 million francs
equipment	33 million francs
exempted social security contributions	1,632 million francs
TOTAL	1,872 million francs
Enterprises	
(apprenticeship tax)	2,200 million francs

Thus, the total running costs of the system amount to 5,817 million francs, with 30% paid by the regional councils, 32% by central government and 38% by enterprises. Compared with the budgets for continuing training and, even more so, education and initial training, this total is still extremely small. Nevertheless, although it is quantitatively modest the apprenticeship system represents a kind of educational model in the vocational training field by virtue of its triple financing (central government/regional councils/enterprises), its mode of instruction based on alternation between the work situation and the training situation and, lastly, the involvement of business and industry and the social partners in its development and administration.

A point to note in this connection is that the social partners, employers and employees representing the various sectors, sit *ex officio* on the CFA board.

The amendment of 8 January 1992, in its turn, is directed at giving fresh impetus to the development of this form of combined education and work by creating the conditions of fruitful co-operation between the sectoral organizations and the national and regional authorities. It provides that policy guidelines on apprenticeship defined at sector level should be the subject of co-operative consultation with central government and the regions, with their implementation possibly giving rise to the conclusion between central government, the regions and the sectoral organizations of target agreements on whose performance the National Joint Commitees on Employment (CNPEs) are kept regularly informed (Art. 10.12). These guidelines may in any event be the subject of national sectoral agreements (Art. 10.13). The new Law of 17 July 1992 explicitly adds this aspect to Article L.933.2 of the Labour Code listing the matters which must be covered by collective bargaining at sector level. It states that the social partners must "define apprenticeship targets, the principles to be followed in terms of sectors, levels and the numbers receiving training and the conditions for the implementation of apprenticeship contracts".

§7. The place and role of the social partners in initial training

It is a specific feature of the French initial training system that the world of work and the social partners who represent it have little presence in the system, essentially because of the importance of general education in the logic of the education system as a whole and the quasi-monopoly of the Ministry of National Education over its administration. They have an effective role in three formal capacities:

(a) The Supreme Council for National Education (CSEN), a consultative body responsible for delivering its opinion to the Minister on methods concerning national education and initial training in other ministries, and public and private education. In particular, it is consulted on all draft laws and decrees. Of its 75 titular members, 13 are intended to represent parents' associations and the employers' associations and trade unions. The role of the latter two is therefore very limited and purely consultative, but they are at least acquainted with documents and major policy guidelines.

(b) The Joint Consultative Committees (CPCs): made up of representatives of the employers' associations and trade unions, the public authorities and individual experts, these formulate opinions and proposals before any form of diploma or course connected with technical education is instituted. They do this mainly on the basis of analyses of training needs and studies of skills carried out by the sectoral organizations. Although their role here, as elsewhere, is purely consultative, they represent an essential channel for the credibility and effectiveness of training courses, especially their recognition by the sectoral organizations during collective bargaining. There are twenty of these CPCs.

(c) The Commission for the Accreditation of formal qualifications and diplomas in technical education: representatives from the world of work sit on this commission in the same capacity as representatives of central administration and the education system.

In official terms, therefore, the role of the social partners is limited. In reality they have a more important motivating power, especially in connection with the upgrading and development of technical education, which would not be credible without their support and in which the authorities are increasingly accepting their active, although not decision-making, participation. However, the major issue in the coming decade in France would certainly appear to be the effective place and influence which the representatives of the economic world may have in the matter of initial training, on essentially three counts.

First, their strategic willingness: this has been evident for more than twenty years in statements made by the representative organizations and, on an official and legal basis, in the texts of the national multi-industry agreements on training and advanced vocational training. Section I of the national agreement of 9 July 1970 covers "provisions relating to initial training", namely, the general education of young people, the organization and supervision of the types of training provided in the vocational context, special provisions relating to the Vocational Studies Certificate (BEP) and, lastly, special provisions relating to apprenticeship. The preamble of the national multi-industry agreement of 3 July 1991 is explicit in this respect. "The signatories have drawn attention to the special responsibility of the social partners with respect to basic technical and vocational training, especially at individual sector level, in the definition of skills and, consequently, of guidelines and priorities on diplomas and validation methods. They have also specified conditions for the entry and follow-up of young people in apprenticeship or training courses in enterprises". Having lain unnoticed for almost twenty years, this concern is once again at the centre of social dialogue.

Second, the upgrading of the apprenticeship model and system, as described here. Although a minority element in quantitative terms, apprenticeship has always represented a kind of reference point in the vocational training field by virtue of the way in which it bases instruction on the alternation of work and training, the rate of placement in jobs of the qualified apprentices it produces, the adaptation of the types of training instituted and the effective participation of the sectoral organizations in its institution and administration. The social partners in the various sectors genuinely feel that the apprenticeship system should serve as a model for technical and vocational education as a whole. In addition, they have recently signed a special agreement (on 7 January 1992) concerning the development of the apprenticeship system, whose upgrading is also, it should be reiterated, one of the priorities of central government as well as a responsibility of the regional councils under general law.

Third, the long-term effects at regional council level of the laws decentralizing apprenticeship, education and initial training and continuing vocational training must be borne in mind. Although their responsibility in regard to education and initial training is confined to the equipment and the construction of lycées (without any powers over teaching or staffing), the real influence of the regional councils is far greater in the form of educational planning which is carried out at the level of each individual region, particularly as regards level V technical and vocational education. In co-operation with central government, the regional councils have to ensure the harmonization and consistency of the various strands and diplomas in the context of the jobs and occupational structure within their particular territory. Thus, in the coming years the regional level will constitute an essential link in the opportunity for the sectoral organizations to exercise an influence, or even a right of inspection, over all the strands of technical and vocational education within initial training.

Lastly, it must be remembered that there is a growing tendency for large enterprises and sectoral organizations to conclude co-operative agreements with Technical University Institutes (IUTs) or scientific and technical universities on the institution and administration of specially adapted training courses, either optional or complementary, in the context of the award of an accredited diploma. On all these counts, the place of the representatives of the world of work in the system is likely to become consolidated in the coming decade, tending to attenuate the historical dichotomy in France between education and production. On the other hand, the question of whether this *rapprochment* will include both sides of industry remains an open one. For the time being, it often comes from the employers alone.

C. Chapter II. Continuing vocational training

§1. History and manner of development

In actual fact, training policies have been mounted by enterprises, associations, popular education movements and denominational or political movements for a very long time. However, the present official institutional system has been developed and governed for more than thirty years on a legislative and contractual basis, according to the following outline:

(a) The Law of 31 December 1959 laid the foundation of the state's commitment in regard to social advancement and vocational training, and set up the financing, administration and co-operative consultation structures which are mostly functioning today.

(b) The national multi-industry agreement of 9 July 1970 and the Law of 16 July 1971 defined the concept of training leave for employees, and the detailed procedures and employers' obligations regarding vocational training. Together, they are often regarded as the founding texts of the continuing vocational training system as it exists today in France.

(c) The Law of 7 January 1983, as part of the series of laws on decentralization transferring powers from central government to the regional authorities, assigned to the regional councils responsibility under general law for vocational training and apprenticeship.

(d) The national multi-industry agreement of 3 July 1991 and the reforming Law of 31 December 1991 introduced a new dimension into French law, namely the principle of "co-investment", whereby employees are required to make a contribution to their employer's training effort in the form of some of their own free time, under conditions that have been defined and negotiated in advance.

Since 1970, the main measures on continuing training, its institutions and the rules which establish them have been generated within the framework of contractual policy between the social partners: in contrast to earlier times and to what is still the case with initial training, the state intervenes in the capacity of legislator only when the representatives of the world of work have signed a national multi-industry agreement: hence, these representatives effectively construct and indirectly regulate the entire system, ranging from exercise of the right to individual training leave for employees, detailed procedures for the enterprise's training plan at the employer's discretion and measures for the absorption of first-time job-seekers into employment to measures for re-training the unemployed, which have all been developed on a joint basis. This is why the continuing training system constitutes a point of reference for the social partners if they ever come to be able to play a more important role in initial training in the future than they do at present.

§2. General structure of the system and apportionment of financing between the actors

The structure of the French vocational training system is multipolar, according to the respective roles of the various decision-makers and finance-providers, as indicated in the diagram in Annex 4.

The three main sources of financing are central government, the regional councils and the enterprise, in proportions which will be defined below. No reliable accounting figures are available at present on the contribution made by individuals in the capacity of employees or job-seekers or on a purely personal basis, or by households, and their contribution is in any case marginal in comparison with the major institutional sources of finance.

The system is based on an extremely dense network of institutions intended to provide training to the various target recipients and to inform them of their entitlement to training and effective opportunities of obtaining it under one of the measures in force. The latter are so numerous that the provision of information and publicity on the entire system has become an absolute necessity. Many of these training structures were established in the 1980s: Local Schemes (Missions locales) and PAIOs (Promotion, Information and Guidance Centres), Job-Start Centres within the framework of first-time employment policy for young people, CARIFs (Training Promotion, Resource and Information Centres) in each region, MIFs (Training Information Centres) and MIPs (Job-Access Schemes) in local labor market areas, and CIBCs (Inter-institutional Skill Assessment Centres).

Central government/region planning contracts are one of the measures of the general Law of 1982 on decentralization. This Law transferred economic planning, formerly the exclusive responsibility of central government, to regional council level, but in order to maintain consistency in national economic development the legislators made provision for this procedure whereby central government and the regional councils decide by agreement to collaborate on common development objectives, region by region. Although these planning contracts cover all aspects of the regional economy, education (initial and continuing training) represents almost a quarter of the total financial appropriation. Planning contracts also lay down key qualitative and strategic guidelines for the future.

The general distribution of financing by type of institutional sector, type of activity and management indicator (number of individuals trained, trainee hours, cost) is shown in Annex 5 for 1990, the latest national figures available.

For the time being, the state is still the major finance-provider for vocational training in France if its role in the financing of training for its own employees is taken into account. If the training of public employees is excluded, enterprises have become the major source of funds and their importance in the system has been increasing constantly for twenty years in both absolute and relative terms (current francs and constant francs).

Although the regional councils possess responsibility under general law for vocational training, they make only a very minor contribution to its financing since the transfer of powers provided for by the law on decentralization was not accompanied by an equivalent transfer of resources; the apprenticeship system, which was entrusted to them, represents only a quasi-marginal proportion of the whole in terms of cost and numbers of beneficiaries.

UNEDIC, the national social protection and insurance body administered jointly by the social partners, has contributed since 1989 to the financing of pay for certain categories of the unemployed under special re-training schemes.

In general, the volume of financing generated by continuing vocational training is close to 100 billion francs, and in reality is certainly higher since this figure includes only expenditure attributable to it under law. This sum represents about 40% of that for initial training and can consequently no longer be regarded as marginal. The initial training/continuing training ratio is therefore changing rapidly in favour of the latter. Since the social partners play a decisive role in continuing training and this is benefiting from a more favourable position, it is only logical that the contractual model which they have developed for continuing training should also serve as a reference point for future developments in initial training.

§3. The market in continuing training

As defined by the Law of 16 July 1971, the training market is very free in France: only a few very simple administrative formalities need to be completed in order to set up a training body, and no requirements regarding experience, competence or prior qualifications have to be met. The system is seen as being regulated by the law of the market. This is why, alongside large publc and private training bodies, a multitude of small and even individual structures can be found which are not always of a permanent nature. It is thought that, generally speaking, 20% of training bodies account for 80% of the business turnover of the total market, while a large number of bodies operate on a very small scale for limited periods or intermittently.

Training bodies, whether governed by public law or private law, are in fact in a situation of competition in a buyer's market. Private bodies are predominant financially (achieving around 60% of all agreed fees for the 1980s). However, the public and para-public apparatus, which is quasi-monopolistic in the case of initial training, also appears to have a very strong presence in continuing vocational training, mainly through large institutions under the tutelage of various Ministries. These include commerce-related groupings (Chambers of Agriculture, of Craft Trades and of Commerce and Industry), the Association for Adult Vocational Training(AFPA) attached to the Ministry of Labour, and bodies coming under the Ministry of National Education: the National College of Advanced Technology (CNAM), the National Centre for Distance Learning (CNED), university departments of continuing education and, above all, the network of GRETAs, which are groupings by geographical area or employment catchment area of initial training structures (essentially lycées and collèges) assigned responsibility for continuing training. Thus, the

GRETA network constitutes a very dense mesh of training-providers over the entire country.

On the private side this is paralleled by the very strong position of another national network, that of the Training Associations (ASFOs), which was established even before 1971 under the aegis of the National Council of French Employers (CNPF) to provide training for the employees of its member enterprises. However, there are no systematic relations between public financing/public training bodies and private financing/private training bodies: a study made in 1990 showed that public training bodies (particularly GRETAs) were achieving an increasingly substantial business turnover with enterprises and that, conversely, private bodies (including ASFOs) were very often involved in publicly financed schemes for the re-training and absorption into employment of young people and the unemployed.

Since 1960, relations between the source of financing and the training body have been governed by two legal procedures:

(a) "conventionnement" (agreed fees), which regulates the payment of teaching costs for employees and job-seekers;
(b) "agrément" (approval), which governs the payment of wages to the individuals receiving training in the case of job-seekers financed by central government or the regional councils.

§4. Role and policy of central government

Although the role of central government in continuing training has been reduced by the growing influence of enterprises over employee training and the process of administrative decentralization with new powers for the regional councils, it is still very significant. In particular, the state aims to finance and manage training for people who are not catered for by the other institutions.

First, the job-seekers aged over 25 who constitute its most important area of intervention: in 1990 the state trained 521,000 of them at a total cost of 14.5 billion francs. A whole series of measures (return-to-work contract, employment training schemes, training for redundant professional and managerial staff, National Employment Agency refresher training courses, redeployment training allowance, re-training agreements, etc.), all of them negotiated with the social partners and some of them (such as the redeployment training allowance and re-training agreements) jointly administered by them within the framework of UNEDIC, have been instituted and are constantly updated. In addition, the French Government has formulated and introduced three Employment Plans, aimed at stimulating economic activity and the hiring of new employees, in which vocational training is an essential element.

Young people emerging from education and initial training without any vocational skills or with inappropriate qualifications constitute central government's second priority target group: in 1990 some 216,000 individuals were trained at a cost of 7.8 billion francs. In common with all European countries, for fifteen years France has been implementing numerous measures for absorbing young people into employment: training courses of various kinds, special contracts of employment incorporating training and government incentive schemes. On 25 October 1983 the social partners signed a national multi-industry agreement relating to this target group midway between initial training and continuing training, giving priority to the contracts of employment formula and government incentive schemes. With the Law of 3 July 1990 the government improved the system by instituting personalized training credits (CFI) for young people, entitling them to acquire particular skills by pursuing a personalized training path within a given geographical area.

Existing employees similarly benefit from state aid: anxious to prevent dismissals rather than to have to remedy their consequences, central government has for ten years pursued a policy of partnership with enterprises and sectoral organizations in regard to redundancy programmes, assistance for the council, human resource planning, updating training and re-training. This takes the form of Aid towards Negotiated Modernization in enterprises, and is targeted principally at small and medium-sized enterprises. In 1990 these measures covered 421,000 employees at a cost of 2.4 billion francs.

Lastly, central government provides training for special groups which are small numerically but pose particular problems for absorption into employment: prisoners, the disabled, immigrants and refugees, and single women. It also ensures, mainly through planning contracts with the regions, the implementation of training measures associated with those economic sectors and activities which have priority in national planning.

Nevertheless, for the past ten years the basic tendency in central government policy has been towards a *rapprochment* with enterprises and sectoral organizations in the attempt to improve the effectiveness of training and the absorption of people into employment, by providing information and involving practitioners and representatives of the world of work more closely in the formulation and implementation of measures.

§5. Role and policies of the regional councils

The regional councils have responsibility under general law for continuing vocational training and apprenticeship. This means that they are able to institute the training policy of their choice, free from any external control, consistent with the regional economic planning which has also devolved upon them as a result of the laws on decentralization. In fact, the regional councils act through two channels corresponding to objectives which may be convergent or divergent.

Firstly, through five-year planning contracts signed with central government. These fix the objectives, means and financing which the two parties decide to allocate to the common economic and development projects for each region. They essentially concern employment, incentives for economic activities, the supply of level V skills, communication infrastructures, land-use planning and both initial and continuing training. The sectoral organizations have no decision-making power in the matter, but depending on the individual region their representatives may participate in project groups and technical committees for formulating the contracts and hence are able to ensure that their needs are taken into account, particularly as regards technological training at levels V and IV.

Secondly, through regional plans for vocational training and apprenticeship which are drawn up for five years and updated annually. Their objectives may diverge widely from those co-contracted with central government. Most regions work on two different and interlinked levels: the level of the development of specific economic areas (particularly local labor markets) and the sectoral level. In the latter case, the representatives of the sectoral organizations are very extensively associated with studies on forecasting and analyses of the training needs in which the regional council invest, since the primary concern of the councils is that the form of training financed by the regional plan should correspond as closely as possible to the skill requirements of enterprises in order to alleviate employment problems. In the context of a wish to achieve an employment-skills-training match at regional and local level, the representatives of the sectoral organizations (or those sectoral organizations which are already properly organized and structured and capable of being forces to be reckoned with) are a key element.

Thus, the *de facto* alliance between regional councils and sectoral organizations in regard to continuing training and apprenticeship, and also to initial training via planning contracts and the formulation of the map of lycée implementation, helps to give these partners a very strong strategic influence which partly outweighs the low level of financial resources granted to the regions by decentralization.

§6. Enterprise financing and policies

If the sums which the state spends on training its own employees are subtracted, enterprises have become the primary source of financing for vocational training in France (see Annex 5). This situation is a new one, because up to the mid-1980s the state had maintained its traditionally predominant role. Since the Law of 16 July 1971, enterprises with 10 or more employees have been obliged to devote a percentage of their wage bill to training for their employees. Even prior to this Law, however, large enterprises and enterprises in leading economic sectors had operated important training policies of their own.

Since the national multi-industry agreement of 3 July 1991 and the Law of 31 December 1991, the total mandatory contribution of 1.4% of the gross wage bill has been divided as follows:

– 0.15% for individual training leave, during which the contract of employment is suspended so that employees can pursue the training of their choice. It is usually for training which is prolonged (more than 800 hours) and/or leads to the acquisition of a particular skill;
– 0.30% for financing forms of combined training-and-work for young people lacking vocational skills and job-seekers;
– 0.95% for financing the employer's training plan, that is all the forms and means of training instituted by the employer to maintain or upgrade the skills of the enterprise's workforce.

Under the same agreement and law, enterprises with fewer than 10 employees are subject to a levy of 0.15%, corresponding to that already in force in the small-scale craft sector.

It must, however, be recognized that this levy represents no more than a formal aspect of financing, and that the real level of expenditure on training is far higher. Given that training is regarded as an intangible investment which is essential to the proper functioning of production, in 1990 enterprises spent, on a national average, 3.20% of their gross wage bill on employee training.

All these forms of expenditure, and training policy more generally, are the subject of consultation with the enterprise's workforce delegates or works council on training policy guidelines, implementation of the current plan and forecasts concerning the plan for the following year. Co-operative consultation is one of the key elements in the perception and implementation of such training in France, particularly for those enterprises which draw up very extensive plans for training over the medium term which are of a strategic nature and innovative in terms of the teaching imparted, and with which employee representatives are for most of the time closely associated. On the other hand, enterprise-level agreements relating to training specifically or indirectly are few in number but quite often highly innovative.

However, financing differs considerably according to the type of enterprise (see Part III below): in percentage terms, large enterprises may spend ten times more than small ones, and for different sectors the ratio is one to seven. The essential problem is still, nevertheless, the development of training in small and medium-sized enterprises, particularly those with fewer than 200 employees, which have limited means for introducing ambitious or innovative plans internally. A number of elements are in place as a potential solution to this problem.

Firstly, the Funds-pooling bodies (see Annex 4), particularly the Training Insurance Funds (FAFs) and Approved Bodies for Combined Training-and-Work (OMAs), which collect the forms of financing which enterprises are unwilling or unable to manage themselves and on which they are entitled to draw. These bodies "mutualize" the available financial resources and to an increasing extent provide advice, analysis of training needs, assessment and policy on training quality for their members. They are managed jointly by the employers' and employees' representatives for each industry or sector, or on a multi-industry basis. This means that. although they receive barely 20% of total enterprise financing, they have the potential to become very important vehicles of innovation for small and medium-sized enterprises, especially in terms of the study and development of training between different enterprises and the concrete application of measures formulated in sector-level agreements.

Secondly, the considerable change in the stance of central government over the past ten years, shifting from a directive and authoritarian view to a strategic view of its role in economic development (see, for example, the work of the Commissariat Général au Plan since 1990). Instead of imposing measures, it now seeks to motivate the economic actors to innovate and to resolve their problems themselves, while providing advice and financing what it sees as meriting top priority. These priorities include aid for small and medium-sized enterprises and the development of training at this level. Assistance for consulting, commitments for the development of training, exemption from social security contributions in respect of special contracts of employment incorporating training and forecasting study contracts with the sectoral organizations have multiplied and represent forms of impetus whose continuation and effects are, moreover, discernible in certain sector-level agreements.

Lastly, these sector-level agreements themselves. Very few in number prior to 1980, and promoted by the Law of 24 February 1984, they multiplied at the end of the 1980s and demonstrated that the social partners were not only aware of the problems of training but also willing to take the initiative themselves in effecting changes and overseeing their implementation more closely. Employers and employees will feel all the more involved and motivated by training when the measures recommended have been negotiated on a joint basis at sector level and do not appear to be imposed from outside by central government for political reasons or by training bodies for commercial reasons. This presupposes that the social partners at sector level are themselves acquainted with the subjects, and from this point of view the content of the agreements described in the present study reveals that they have already adopted the specialized terminology of the training sector.

It would therefore seem that, in parallel with the ambitious and long-term training policies of large enterprises and groups which function independently, sector-level agreements may be the trigger for training projects involving new types of partnership and contracting between the various actors: small and medium-sized enterprises/sectoral organizations/central government/regional councils.

§7. The place and role of the social partners in continuing vocational training

In contrast to the case of initial training, where their role is a minor one, the social partners occupy a central and determining position in the continuing vocational training system, which is only logical since the development of this system has from the outset been closely linked with the world of work. Their role takes effect at four different levels:

(a) They contribute, via collective bargaining, to the development of the law on continuing training. This is particularly true of national multi-industry agreements but also, to a lesser extent, of certain sector-level and enterprise-level agreements (see Part III below).

(b) They are associated, in a consultative capacity, with those central government and regional authorities which are responsible for implementing training policies. For instance, there is formal provision for their participation in the following bodies:

– National Council for Vocational Training (and its subsidiary bodies), which is consulted by the Ministry of Labour and the Prime Minister on all new policies, measures and guidelines concerning vocational training and apprenticeship.

– Regional Economic and Social Committee: although its powers and responsibilities have bearing on all areas of economic, social and cultural life, its action in training matters (initial and continuing) is important in terms of studies, diagnostics and forecasting. Among other things, it is consulted at various stages in the procedures for formulating regional plans and central government/region planning contracts.

– Regional Committee for Vocational Training (COREF): this assembly gives an opinion on all agreements and authorizations for training activities in each region financed by central government or the regional council. It is presided over in turn by the Prefect of the region or the Chairman of the regional council. Although a consultative body, it is a central link in the system in terms of information, since all documentation on activities involving even partial public financing (such as special employment training contracts for young people) pass through its hands. Agreements between central government or region and sectoral organizations also fall within its sphere of competence.

– Département Committee for Vocational Training (CODEF): this fulfills the same functions as the COREF, but at département level. Its role has been lessened for the past ten years as a result of the decentralization of vocational training and apprenticeship, but recent measures on de-concentration, *i.e.* delegation of the administration of central government policies to département level, particularly schemes for the young people and the unemployed, have now given it renewed vigour.

(c) The social partners themselves undertake the monitoring of agreements negotiated within the Joint Committees on Employment (see Part II below), direct administration of policies negotiated on a joint administration basis and monitoring of specialist bodies (see Part II below).

(d) Lastly, within the enterprise, the works council or workforce delegates are provided with information and consulted on the implementation of training in the enterprise (see Part II below).

D. Conclusions

Over the past decade or two the economic world and hence the social partners who represent it, traditionally distanced from the French education system
for historical reasons, notably the cardinal and driving role of the state, have
effected a significant *rapprochement* with the world of training. This development will undoubtedly go still farther. Several elements would appear to point
in this direction.

First, the tendency over the long term for initial training and continuing
training to be viewed not in an isolated or indeed contradictory manner, but as
part of a continuum in which finance-providers, regulators and practitioners
will need to co-ordinate their efforts better in order to meet the unprecedented
educational challenges of the coming decades, achieve economies of scale, and
ensure the genuine opportunity of access to education and training for every
individual, employees or otherwise, throughout their lifetime, thereby bringing
the reality into closer conformity with the law. In this view of things, and as a
continuation of what has already been observed for the past fifteen years, it is
the institutional practices of continuing training, with the preponderant role
played here by the social partners, which will tend to "pull after them" the
practices of initial training in terms of strategies for educational development
and planning, administration of integrated training systems and methods of
social regulation.

Second, the need to achieve a better match between training, both initial and
continuing, and the characteristics of employment, so that existing job vacancies can be filled, first-time job-seekers will have less difficulty in gaining
access to employment, and there will be less need for the re-training and re-
skilling of employees. This is particularly true of the increased emphasis on
apprenticeship and the technical and vocational strands in education and initial
training, the human resource planning practices in the large private or public
groups with which the trade unions are generally associated and, above all, the
schemes for the absorption into employment of young people with low skill
levels, where the coherence and closely detailed management of the employment-skills-training link are central elements in absorption into employment
and stability of employment. Such practices cannot be put into effect without
the active participation of the representatives of the world of work.

Lastly, as the third and possibly the determining element in that it may bring
together the first two, the concrete and long-term effects of the decentralization of both initial vocational training and continuing vocational training.
These reforms, which are fundamental in the French administrative system
although they have not yet been fully implemented, are still far from getting
into their stride and are unlikely to produce their real effects until the next
decade. Some of these effects are certainly still unforeseeable, particularly as
regards education and initial training where the transfer of responsibility to
elected bodies at various levels of the regional authorities augurs difficult rela-

tions with the Ministry of National Education in the future. Nevertheless, the overriding trend which in some ways is beginning to emerge is that problems of educational planning need to be dealt with at regional and even local level, following the questionable validity and relative failure of centralized national planning. From this point of view, a real matching of training policies to sectoral policies can be achieved if the social partners in the various industries are mobilized and if the state, decentralized into its various component parts, is willing and able to institute a proper partnership. Collaboration between certain industries (such as tourism and hotels and catering) and regional councils or employment catchment area committees is already a reality in several regions.

These three factors (linking of initial training and continuing training, relationship between employment and training, and effective decentralization) will combine and consolidate to give the economic world and its representatives greater weight in educational matters than in the past and, hence, to shift the position of the state in its historical role as the predominant actor, although without in any way calling into question the legitimacy of its action. In these circumstances, there is no doubt that regulatory mechanisms of vocational training systems which are based on contracting, and in particular collective bargaining, will continue to develop. The same is true of methods of administration which are based on co-operation, and more particularly on joint, or even multipartite, principles.

E. ANNEXES

Annex 1:   General structure of education and initial training in France

Annex 2:   Distribution of pupil and student numbers in education and initial training by type and level

Annex 3:   Correspondence between employment levels and education and training levels

Annex 4:   Functional diagram of the continuing training system in France

Annex 5:   Apportionment of financing for continuing training in France

ANNEX 1

GENERAL STRUCTURE OF EDUCATION AND INITIAL TRAINING IN FRANCE

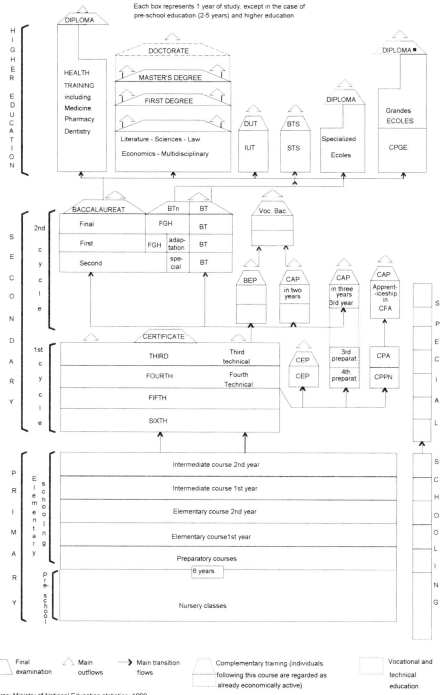

* Each box represents 1 year of study, except in the case of pre-school education (2-5 years) and higher education

Source: Ministry of National Education statistics, 1990

ANNEX 2

DISTRIBUTION OF PUPIL AND STUDENT NUMBERS IN
EDUCATION AND INITIAL TRAINING BY TYPE AND LEVEL

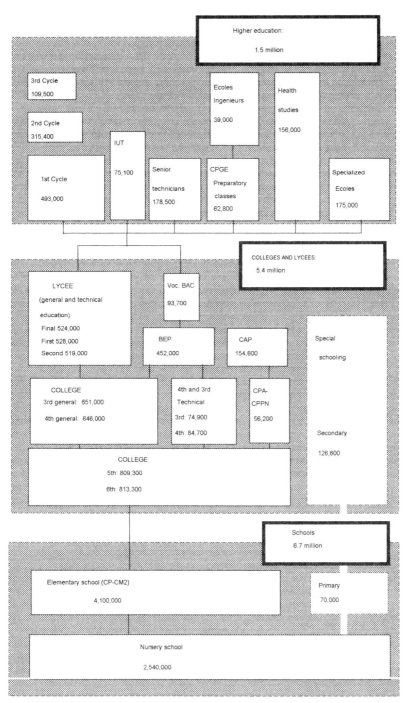

ANNEX 3

CORRESPONDENCE BETWEEN EMPLOYMENT LEVELS
AND EDUCATION AND TRAINING LEVELS

LEVELS	DEFINITIONS
I and II	Personnel occupying jobs normally requiring education and training of a level equal to or higher than that of a first degree or of the Ecoles d'Ingénieurs.
III	Personnel occupying jobs normally requiring education and training up to the level of Advanced Technician Certificate (BTS) or diploma of the University Institutes of Technology (DUT) and of the first cycle of higher education (DEUG).
IV	Personnel occupying supervisory jobs or possessing a qualification of a level equivalent to the Baccalauréat, the Technician Baccalauréat (BTn) or Technician Certificate (BT), or the Vocational Baccalauréat.
V	Personnel occupying jobs normally requiring a level of education and training equivalent to the Vocational Studies Certificate (BEP) or Certificate of Vocational Competence (CAP) and, by assimilation, the Certificate of Adult Vocational Training (CFPA) 1st stage.
Vb	Individuals occupying jobs presupposing a short (1-year maximum) form of training leading to a Vocational Education Certificate (CEP) or any other certificate of the same kind.
VI	Personnel occupying jobs requiring no education or training beyond the completion of compulsory schooling.

ANNEX 4

FUNCTIONAL DIAGRAM OF THE CONTINUING TRAINING SYSTEM IN FRANCE

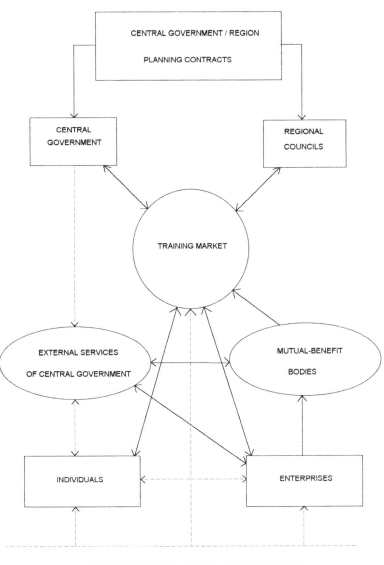

CENTRAL GOVERNMENT / REGION

PLANNING CONTRACTS

CENTRAL GOVERNMENT

REGIONAL COUNCILS

TRAINING MARKET

EXTERNAL SERVICES OF CENTRAL GOVERNMENT

MUTUAL-BENEFIT BODIES

INDIVIDUALS

ENTERPRISES

INFORMATION, RECEPTION AND GUIDANCE STRUCTURES

ANNEX 5

APPORTIONMENT OF FINANCING FOR CONTINUING TRAINING IN FRANCE

		INDIVIDUALS RECEIVING TRAINING (millions)	TRAINING HOURS (millions)	COST (thousand million francs)
CENTRAL GOVERNMENT	Continuing training	1.56	386	21.8
	Absorption of young people into employment	0.36	–	4.8
	Apprenticeship	–	–	1.9
	Training of state employees	1.9	52	17.8
CENTRAL GOVERNMENT	TOTAL	3.78	438	46.3
REGIONS	Continuing training	0.43	124	3.5
	Apprenticeship	0.24	–	2.0
REGIONS	TOTAL	0.67	124	5.5
ENTERPRISES	TOTAL	3.28	270	37.9
UNEDIC	TOTAL	–	–	3.6
GENERAL	TOTAL	7.73	832	93.3

Source: Draft Finance Law, 1992

PART II: CONTRACTUAL POLICY ON CONTINUING VOCATIONAL TRAINING: LEGAL FRAMEWORK AND MAIN RESULTS

A. Introductory remarks

(1) Collective bargaining occupies a key position in the French continuing vocational training system.

Its intervention makes itself felt at multi-industry level, sector level and enterprise level. In many instances it is extended through the joint administration of "social institutions" concerned with training (which is undertaken by the social partners themselves) and through the information and consultation rights conferred by law on the elected representatives of the workforce within the enterprise, which are exercised in conjunction with the intervention of the social partners.

Although the social partners enjoy complete autonomy in all decision-making that takes place within the process of collective bargaining as laid down by the Labour Code, their sphere of intervention cannot really be isolated from that of central government, training-providers and enterprises. The decisions taken by each of these actors, and the measures they apply in their respective spheres of autonomy, all interact extensively with each other. Such interaction is, furthermore, methodically encouraged and organized by French law, thereby lending a certain originality to the French continuing training system in the European context.

(2) The involvement of collective bargaining in vocational training is not a long-standing phenomenon in France. In any meaningful sense, it began only twenty years ago with the growing awareness of the problem shown by the social partners, strongly encouraged by the public authorities with appropriate supportive measures. What is more, it is an evolving process which has not yet reached its limits and in which the issues involved are considerable.

Thus, the respective roles of central government and the social partners may shift farther in the direction of the latter. Also, bargaining at sector level could become more active than it is at present, and likewise bargaining at enterprise level, which is still relatively marginal. As regards the matters covered, although the vocational training of both existing employees and job-seekers and also apprenticeship are now largely covered, initial vocational training is still outside the scope of collective bargaining.

The issues involved are numerous and considerable: matters covered by collective bargaining include organization of the right of access to training for employees, the distribution of available financial resources and the way in which they are administered, the certification of skills acquired through such training and its recognition in the classification and qualification system, and the monitoring of training provision.

(3) The systemic nature of the organization of vocational training in France and the ways in which the social partners also influence the system via mechanisms other than straightforward collective bargaining make it seem useful to start by describing the intervention of the social partners in vocational training through collective bargaining, and then to describe their intervention via other mechanisms such as joint administration and co-operative consultation between the employer and the elected representatives of the workforce.

B. CHAPTER I. THE LEGAL FRAMEWORK OF COLLECTIVE BARGAINING

The legal framework of collective bargaining as applied to training consists of the provisions of general law concerning bargaining (Section III, Book I of the Labour Code) and specific provisions contained in Book IX concerning vocational training, supplemented by the provisions of Book III concerning employment (Art. 322.7).

§1. The general law of collective bargaining

Section III of Book I of the Labour Code defines "the rules governing exercise of the right of employees to collective negotiation of the entire range of their terms and conditions of employment and working conditions and their *social guarantees*" (Art. L. 131-1, Labour Code). Although continuing training may be connected with terms and conditions of employment and working conditions, it is above all a "social guarantee" in the sense given to it by this text: the parliamentary debates on the Law of 13 July 1971 which introduced the concept of the social guarantee include continuing training among them. "What is important is that the words *social guarantees* should be interpreted sufficiently broadly to include the problems of guarantee of employment, unemployment benefit, supplementary pensions, vocational training and continuing education without its being possible to draw up an exhaustive list" (Journal Officiel, National Assembly Debates, 15 May 1971, p. 1914).

Also, continuing training features in the list of mandatory clauses for those collective agreements to which the official extension procedure may be applied.

These agreements must contain provisions on: "Details of the organization and functioning of apprenticeship, vocational training and continuing training in the sector in question...." (Art. L. 133-5 (8), Labour Code).

The same Article specifies, in regard to equality between men and women in employment, that training and career advancement are among the corrective measures to be implemented in order to remedy these inequalities (Arts. L. 135-5(9) and L. 123-3-1, Labour Code).

Such agreements must contain "the essential information needed to determine job classifications and skill levels, and in particular references to vocational diplomas or their equivalences provided these diplomas have been in existence for more than one year (Arts. L. 133-5(3) and 132.12, Labour Code).

Lastly, collective agreements on employment may provide for the organization of long-term training activities aimed at easing the adaptation of employees to changes in employment in the enterprise (Art. L. 322-7).

§2. The place of collective bargaining in Book IX of the Labour Code concerning continuing training

(a) The core of the system consists in an obligation on the organizations bound by a sector-level agreement to meet at least every five years for negotiations on the priorities, objectives and means of vocational training for employees (Art. L. 933-2).

These negotiations mainly relate to the following points:

- the nature of training activities and their order of priority;
- recognition of skills acquired as a result of training activities;
- the means granted to trade union delegates and works council members to enable them to fulful their function as regards training;
- vocational training aspects of arrangements for the entry and integration of young people into employment in enterprises;
- training activities to be implemented for the benefit of lowest-skilled employees to assist their career development;
- the definition of training activities aimed at ensuring equality of access to vocational training for men and women, and the conditions of their implementation;
- in the case of enterprises whose expenditure on employee training is at least equal to the minimum statutory obligation or to that fixed by a sector-level agreement on the participation of employers in the financing of continuing vocational training, the conditions of enforcement of any financial clauses which are agreed between employer and employee prior to the commencement of certain training activities and which take effect in the event of resignation (payments received on the basis of these clauses are passed on by the enterprise to the financing of activities within its training plan);
- the search for appropriate solutions to the special problems of training in small and medium-sized enterprises, particularly those with fewer than ten employees;
- the possible impact on training needs of changes in the content and organization of work and changes in working hours;
- the impact on training needs and activities of the development of French business activity abroad;
- detailed arrangements for the implementation by enterprises of the provisions of any sector-level agreement which may result from these negotiations.

(b) Book IX contains other provisions on collective bargaining which illustrate the close intermeshing of statutory and contractual sources in vocational training law.

For instance, the Training Insurance Funds (FAFs) are set up on the basis of collective agreements (Art. R. 960-36, Labour Code), as are also the Manpower and Training Associations (AMOFs), which combine part-time work and training (Art. L. 982-5).

The legislators go so far as to recognize, in the case of individual training leave, that negotiated rules take precedence over administrative provisions, which apply only where no negotiated rules exist (Art. L. 931-12, Labour Code).

C. Chapter II. Levels of bargaining on vocational training

§1. National multi-industry level

(a) The national multi-industry agreement of 3 July 1991 on vocational training and further training, which was negotiated on the twentieth anniversary of the multi-industry agreement of 9 July 1970 and to which the official extension procedure has been applied, constitutes the cornerstone of the French continuing vocational training system.

It laid the foundations of individual training leave in 1970 and established guidelines on training provision for young people and apprentices and for employees threatened by redundancy. Between 1970 and 1990 the basic text was supplemented by seven amendments or protocols, ending in the updated new agreement of 3 July 1991. Over these twenty years, individual training leave underwent profound changes, combined training-and-work formulas were brought within the sphere of competence of collective bargaining, and joint administration of vocational training (as a "social guarantee") was recognized as making good sense and its scope of application was broadened. Sector-level bargaining increased to some extent as a result of supportive legislation, and the rules of social dialogue at enterprise level in regard to training were clarified. The information, consultation and participation rights of the elected workforce representatives, the works council and workforce delegates, were expanded, although the employer's autonomy and managerial authority remained intact.

(b) Multi-industry bargaining on training takes place exclusively at national level. It is, however, continued down to regional multi-industry level in the form of the Regional Multi-industry Joint Committees on Employment (COPIREs), which unite the social partners in dealing with regional employment and training problems and co-operative consultation with regional authorities.

Also, some Training Insurance Funds (FAFs) exist which are set up under framework agreements at regional multi-industry level, but they are rare.

(c) The geographical coverage of the agreement is national. Its scope of application in terms of the persons and occupations covered derives from the nature of the contracting parties. Consequently, all of the enterprises which belong to one of the employers' organizations affiliated to the National Council of French Employers (CNPF) or the General Confederation of Small and Medium-sized Enterprises (CGPME) are covered by it, except for any which expressly requested to be excluded when the agreement was signed. Such was the case when the agreement of 9 July 1970 was signed.

The agreement of 3 July 1991, which initially covered only all enterprises belonging to CNPF, CGPME or the Union of Small Craft Businesses (UPA), was subsequently also made binding on all enterprises falling within its occupational scope which do not belong to the signatory employers' organizations, under the official extension procedure provided for in Article L. 133-8 *et seq.* of the Labour Code.

However, extension in the real sense, which constitutes one of the unique features of the French continuing training system, is attributable to the legislators themselves, who since 1970 have translated into legislation the essence of the outcome of collective bargaining by the social partners at national multi-industry level. By incorporating it into a universally applicable law, they axiomatically settled the question of the agreement's scope of application. The Law of 31 December 1991 was no exception to this rule, because it extended the applicability of the agreement of 3 July 1991.

Specific agreements have been concluded in sectors which do not fall within the sphere of competence of the signatory employers' organizations (CNPF and CGPME). Examples include the agricultural sector, retail and small craft businesses sector, non-profit-making sector, temporary work, hospital sector, etc. All of these texts are essentially based on the main topics of the multi-industry agreement, which is the cornerstone of vocational training law, but cover aspects specific to the occupations concerned: replacement of employees during training, mutualization of financing, etc.

The virtues of collective bargaining on training have been recognized by the state itself in its capacity of employer, resulting in the negotiation of a framework agreement and implementation agreements for each Ministry.

§2. Sector level

(a) Up to the early 1980s, sector-level bargaining on vocational training was not significant as such. Agreements negotiated in the industries covered by the national multi-industry agreement were merely a reproduction of existing statutory rules or multi-industry provisions, or declarations of intent. However, the social partners were not inactive at this level. They participated in the Joint Committees on Employment on which the multi-industry agreement had conferred responsibility for the approval of training courses deemed useful for the industry in question and its employees, and in the Training Insurance Funds. Also, some sector-level agreements on job classifications or employment policy contained provisions relating to training.

(b) In 1984 the legislators took action to revitalize sector-level bargaining in the form of a legal incentive to bargain on training, complementing the incentive introduced in 1982 by the "Auroux" laws relating to wages and job classifications (Art. L 132.12).

Under the former Article L. 932-2 of the Labour Code, the social partners were required to open negotiations in the sector concerned within a period of 12 months after the promulgation of the law. Failing this, enterprises in sectors not covered by an agreement were under an obligation to bargain. The law gave a non-exhaustive list of compulsory bargaining topics.

The effect of this incentive was to trigger bargaining in almost all sectors.

Although as a consequence the social partners became familiar with this new field, in qualitative terms the results of bargaining on training were still modest at the end of the 1980s.

(c) Results for 1985-1990

At the end of 1985, 65 agreements had been signed pursuant to Article L. 932-2 of the Labour Code. The extension procedure was used for 31 of them. Most economic sectors were affected.

On the whole, the content of bargaining remains confined to broad generalities. This is true as regards the nature of training activities and their order of priority, responsibility for which is often delegated to the Joint Committee on Employment for the industry concerned.

Provisions are also "general" as regards the recognition of skills acquired through training activities: the award of certificates to trainees who have successfully passed tests, accompanied by priority for possible promotion. No agreements actually make such "priority" amount to a right to promotion. It was particularly expected that bargaining would help to achieve the recognition of training. As early as 1971, the legislators had expressed the wish that during the negotiation of collective agreements for which the extension procedure might be used the parties should specify "the essential information needed to determine occupational classifications and skill levels, and in particular references to vocational diplomas provided these diplomas have been in existence for more than one year". In 1976 and 1982 the social partners themselves had taken up this issue, recommending that collective agreements should specify ways of recognizing the skills acquired by an employee who has obtained such a vocational diploma at the end of a training course and has subsequently been assigned to a post corresponding to its special nature.

In this respect, the results of bargaining carried out in compliance with the obligation imposed by the Rigout law of 24 February 1984 were uneven. Apart from a few incentive mechanisms such as bonuses, indexation points or priority consideration for any job vacancies corresponding to the new skill level acquired, the general rule is still that collective agreements contain no automatic recognition of skills acquired through continuing training.

A number of agreements do, however, grant paid time off to workforce representatives, including the members of training committees.

As regards the absorption of young people into employment, all of the agreements describe combined training-and-work formulas and the details of their implementation. The role of the tutors is usually emphasized. Most agreements name the body responsible for collecting the sums due under the levies on employers for apprenticeship and continuing vocational training.

From 1986 to 1990 there was less bargaining activity than in 1985: only 18 sector-level agreements were recorded in 1986, 28 in 1987, 37 in 1988, 24 in 1989 and 20 in 1990.

(d) The five-yearly bargaining process instituted by the Laignel law of 4 July 1990 was relaunched with the national multi-industry agreement of 3 July 1991 and the Law of 31 December 1991, without any great success. The Ministry of Labour recorded only 25 collective agreements for 1991 specifically relating to training. Analysis of these texts reveals two major, albeit conventional, features: the emphasis placed on the concerted definition of training policies, and joint administration of training mainly as regards financing and mutualization techniques.

It must, however, be stressed that specific agreements on training do not represent the whole of the result of sector-level bargaining in this field. Other agreements on employment, technological change, job classification or working conditions frequently contain a strong " training" component.

For instance, three agreements were concluded pursuant to the Law of 2 August 1989 (Article 322.7 of the Labour Code) in the metals sector (23 January 1991), the chemical industry (15 January 1991) and the milk industry (15 February 1991). They provide for long-term training measures to assist the adaptation of employees to changes in employment.

These three agreements stress the need for human resource planning at sector or enterprise level and include measures directed at employees who experience difficulty in adapting to changes in employment.

Similarly, in the context of bargaining on job classifications some industries adopt the objective of offering employees career development prospects making use of skills acquired through training (e.g. metals sector agreement)

These innovatory trends are confirmed by the main findings of the case-studies carried out in eight sectors for the purposes of the present study:

* The vitality of the principle of joint administration as a continuation of bargaining is strongly evidenced, whether it is founded in formal institutional contexts (Training Insurance Funds (FAFs), Approved Funds-pooling Bodies for Combined Training-and-Work (OMAs), training bodies) or in more informal systems such as the Joint Committees on Employment (CPEs), in any event constituting the concrete application of negotiated rules. The particular form such co-operation takes depends on the tradition and individual features of the industry concerned (predominance of small and medium-sized enterprises, history of industrial relations, special nature of training provision, etc.).
* There is a definite correlation between the volume of bargaining and incentives provided by the state in the form of forecasting study contracts and agreements for a training development commitment. Tools for gathering information on employment and skills backed by state support provide the bargaining parties with good "grist for the mill".
* Several sectors (e.g. building, metals) are adopting a global approach to training, establishing links between initial vocational training, apprenticeship and continuing training. This approach is discernible in the "programmatic" provisions of the agreements concerned.

* The need to recruit and to retain the loyalty of a skilled workforce, particularly young people, has prompted certain industries (*e.g.* building, food distribution, textiles) to pay special attention to policies on the absorption and integration of workers into the industry in question, and on paths to obtaining skills (tutors, apprenticeship masters, certification of skills acquired, movement between different forms of training, etc.). The same concern is evident with respect to older employees in the form of "re-skilling paths" enabling them to adapt to changes within their particular industry (textiles, building, metals).
* Without doubt, however, it is the certification of skills acquired through certain types of training leading to level V to III qualifications which represents the major innovation resulting from bargaining. The social partners' intention to gain better control over qualifications is clear in two of the industries included in our sample: chemicals and metals.

Another innovation, encountered in the building industry in particular, is the recognition of skills acquired through experience, *i.e.* not certificated by a diploma of any kind.

§3. Enterprise level

The obligation to bargain within the enterprise that was imposed by the legislators in 1984 for cases where there has been no sector-level bargaining has had little effect on the development of enterprise-level bargaining on training. In enterprises where social dialogue on training exists, it takes place by virtue of the exhaustive powers of information and consultation which the law confers on the works council.

(a) Results for 1990

However, bargaining on training at enterprise level is not entirely absent, since the social partners have complete freedom to negotiate on it if they wish and if conditions so indicate.

According to the Ministry of Labour's assessment of collective bargaining for 1990, 131 enterprise-level agreements relating to training were negotiated in that year, representing 2% of all enterprise-level agreements concluded on all issues (pay, working conditions, etc.). Analysis of these texts reveal three main trends:

* Training is a tool of company policy. Agreements which reflect this policy deal with all aspects of training (enterprise training plan, individual training leave, personal initiative, etc.) and often link training, employment and career or grading prospects. They originate from large and medium-sized enterprises which are motivated to devote special efforts to training. Some agreements include an undertaking to devote a substantially larger proportion of their wage bill to training than the rate stipulated by law.
* It is implemented in a context of concerted co-operation: the respective roles of management, workforce representatives and employees themselves are often specified.

* There is a growing tendency to personalize training. This represents a response to the dual concern to define training needs more clearly and to motivate the individual concerned, as a promise of efficiency.

The personalization of training is taking effect not only within the context of the enterprise's training plan but also as regards individual training leave and other personal projects apart from such leave. The distinction between these three categories is tending to become blurred.

Within the context of the enterprises's training plan, some agreements encourage employees to define a personal training project which, if approved by the enterprise, will be funded by the latter. In an Alsace brasserie studied, this right will be implemented in the year following such a request. And an enterprise in the aircraft industry allocates 10% of its training budget to funding such initiatives (for the benefit of a particular category of employees to whom long-term training is offered).

To encourage employees to take advantage of individual training leave, agreements contain measures such as:

– assistance from the training department in preparing and presenting documentation for applications to financing bodies;
– payment of expenses (documentation, accommodation, travel, placement, etc) or of an advance. If an application is rejected by the Fund for the Administration of Individual Training Leave (FONGECIF), there is provision for financial assistance or possible inclusion in the enterprise's training plan.

Apart from the enterprise's training plan and individual training leave, some agreements support personal projects. An enterprise in the food industry which was studied pays expenses and grants five days off for forms of training leading to diplomas even if they are unconnected with the employee's particular job and take place outside working hours. And an enterprise in the aircraft industry grants time off amounting to 38 hours per year and allows adjustments to working hours.

(b) Results for 1991

The 1991 findings confirm these same trends.

Although only 131 enterprise-level or establishment-level agreements were signed during 1991, this was the same number as in 1990 and the overall trend was on the increase in comparison with the preceding years (88 in 1989, 56 in 1988, and 97 in 1987).

According to the Ministry of Labour, analysis of these agreements yields the following indications:

– Agreements frequently relate to employment or job classifications (60%) and mostly originate from large enterprises (43% were concluded in enterprises with more than 500 employees), in many instances subsidiaries of public enterprises in the metals industry (33% of agreements) or the banking sector. Medium-sized enterprises tend rather to sign specific "vocational training" agreements. A number of agreements do not cover the content of training but confine themselves to its financing (increase in the proportion of the wage bill) or organization (use and support of individual training leave).

– There is a growing tendency to make training an integral element of human resource management policies (40% of agreements), even though more *ad hoc* forms of training connected with adaptation to changes in jobs still predominate. The latter include refresher training as a preliminary to training leading to a new skill (14%), but still mostly consist of training to improve adaptation abilities (44%) or training in new techniques (25%).

– Training tends to play a direct part in the forward management of careers and skills: 25% of agreements deal with career development and 14% of training activities are intended for employees being transferred or re-trained, or those whose jobs are at risk.

– There are some instances of the individualization of training, by means of preliminary interviews before the commencement of training or methods of skill appraisal (14%).

– There are still few provisions on the internal organization of training. Some 25% of agreements state that a part of training will take place internally, but detailed arrangements are almost non-existent: 11 agreements deal with this problem.

– Ways of validating skills acquired through training are becoming more diversified. In addition to state education diplomas (14 agreements), new forms of certification are appearing such as sector-level qualification certificates (13 agreements) or even skill audit (or other equivalents).

– Recognition of skills acquired through training, for which there is still little provision (25% of agreements), is reflected either in higher pay or in eligibility for access to a more highly skilled job (2 agreements guarantee such access).

– Provisions relating to training outside working hours (or explicitly to "co-investment") are rare (2 agreements).

– The involvement of the social partners is significant (33% of agreements) notably through the works council's training committee.

D. Chapter III. Joint administration

§1. Definition

Joint administration is the term used to designate the system of administration whereby trade unions and employers' associations decide to administer a social guarantee (in this case, continuing training) on a joint basis. In its simplest form, it implies strictly parity composition of the management bodies of the institutions concerned. The employers' college and trade union college are each composed of an equal number of representatives; they have equal powers, and the presidency of the management board alternates between them. Generally speaking, joint bodies are created on the basis of a shared decision, which is itself taken jointly (collective agreement). This is true of the Training Insurance Funds (FAFs) and Funds for the Administration of Individual Training Leave (FONGECIFs), but is not an essential condition. For instance, the Training Associations (ASFOs) are created by unilateral decision of one or more employers' associations, and have adopted joint administration for only some of their activities.

The pluralism of French trade unions lends joint administration a particular image, but has not prevented its adoption for various social guarantees such as unemployment insurance or supplementary pensions. These two have indisputably served as models influencing the establishment of the joint administration principle in the field of training.

Joint administration is an expression of the battle for power between employers' associations and trade unions. In the matter of training, their competing priorities include the purpose of training (what kind of training should be given preference and hence financing?), the interests of the enterprise versus those of the employees, the choice of training-providers (public or private), and the recognition of skills acquired through training (formal qualification, diplomas, certificates, etc.).

From the employers' viewpoint, joint administration of training should be confined to carefully delimited areas. The autonomy of the employer's managerial authority must not be weakened by the application of the joint administration principle to training. This is the reason behind the employers' rejection of the idea that the Training Insurance Funds should become generalized and also their rejection of any interference by joint structures in enterprise training policies.

The trade unions themselves are in fact divided on the matter of joint administration and its use, and in any event are not in favour of its use at enterprise level in the form of co-management of training.

Joint administration may also be in the common interest of both sides, who may find themselves united by it against the public authorities, particularly in defending its autonomy. The establishment of the Joint Committees on Individual Training Leave (COPACIFs) and Funds for the Administration of Individual Training Leave (FONGECIFs) was one such case.

§2. Training Insurance Funds

(a) Training Insurance Funds (FAFs) are marked by several distinctive features:

- They are created by collective agreement (compulsory membership agreement or framework agreement allowing voluntary membership). Their geographical and occupational coverage may therefore be as varied as that of collective agreements.
- They are administered on a joint basis, *i.e.*their management board must be composed of equal numbers of employer and union representatives.
- Their task is to "assist the development of training by using their resources to this end (trainees' pay, training costs, studies, information, increasing the awareness of employees and employers, etc.)".
- They are authorized to mutualize the contributions paid to them by member enterprises, *i.e.* to decide how to allocate all or part of their resources regardless of who has paid particular contributions.
- They possess legal personality.
- They are under the control of the public authorities: their creation is subject to official approval and their operation and financial administration are subject to the authority of the bodies which oversee vocational training.

(b) The FAFs are financed from contributions paid by enterprises. They may receive public subsidies (Arts. R. 964-14 and L. 950-2(2)). Financial revenues generated by these deposited funds are governed by the same regulations as the funds and are allocated by the management board. Lastly, like all legal persons the FAFs may receive donations and legacies.

In point of fact, the contributions paid by enterprises represent the bulk of their resources. As a rule, the amount of the contribution is fixed by the FAF.

(c) Sphere of competence

According to the original texts, intervention by the FAFs was intended to be for the exclusive benefit of the employees of member enterprises. The financing of training leave was considered to be their main purpose. In addition, they provided advice, information and technical assistance to the employer for the implementation of training policy.

In practice, things turned out somewhat differently. The priority which the FAFs were to have given to training leave was rarely translated into reality, the bulk of their resources being allocated to financing activities deriving from enterprise training plans.

Moreover, as the employment situation worsened the demand for financing for the training of job-seekers intensified and the boundary which the legislators originally intended to keep clearly marked between training insurance for employees in existing jobs and unemployment-training insurance for those without jobs became more blurred, with the result that the FAFs were prompted to contribute to the financing of training for job-seekers.

Lastly, the considerable growth in unemployment among young people and the training measures introduced as a result gave some FAFs a new sphere of intervention in the form of combined training-and-work schemes.

(d) Assessment

Of the 96 FAFs which exist, 48 are at national level, 23 at regional or inter-regional level, 20 at inter-depártement, depártement or local level and 5 at enterprise level. In 1990 membership of FAFs comprised 86,938 enterprises with ten or more employees, and 278,246 enterprises with fewer than ten employees representing a total of 486,000 employees (170,000 of them in the agricultural seector).

As regards activities under enterprise training plans, the FAFs provided total or partial funding for training for 588,071 employees in 1990, representing 30.5 million training hours. In addition, they financed 8,000 periods of individual training leave (totalling 51.4 million francs) and 3,060 job-seekers (totalling 27.2 million francs).

Apart from the actual financial administration of fully or partly mutualized resources, the FAFs help to organize the training policies of member enterprises. This is particularly the case with small and medium-sized enterprises, for which the FAFs act as a shared training service, helping to analyse sectoral training needs and to formulate and implement training policies.

§3. Joint bodies with responsibility for individual training leave

In 1982, the social partners decided that part of the enterprises' financial contribution should be allocated to the financing of individual training leave, and that it should be administered by joint bodies created for the purpose. At present, there are 67 joint bodies with responsibility for financing individual training leave: 31 Funds for the Administration of Individual Training Leave (FONGECIFs), for which it represents their sole function, and 36 Training Insurance Funds (FAFs), for which it is one activity amongst others.

In 1990, the resources allocated to individual training leave by these joint bodies represented 3.74 billion francs. This provided funding for 25,600 applications for individual training leave out of a total of 38,500 applications. The average length of such training courses is 876 hours, and they are mostly for the purpose of occupational advancement.

This financing mechanism represents concrete application of the principle of the right to paid educational leave recommended by the ILO in 1975. Consequently, it is directed personally at the employee who benefits from a period of individual training leave, without any intervention by the enterprise.

§4. Approved Funds Pooling bodies with responsibility for combined training-and-work schemes

There are 199 such Approved Funds Pooling Bodies (OMAs), which administer on a joint basis the funds they receive from enterprises for combined training-and-work schemes for young people (involving special employment training contracts variously called *contrat de qualification, contrat d'adaption and contrat d'orientation*).

In 1990 their resources totalled 7,650 billion francs, and were used to finance the training costs incurred by enterprises under special employment training contracts signed with young people aged 16-25.

Unlike the Funds for the Administration of Individual Training Leave (FONGECIFs), these OMAs deal only with the enterprises concerned, which have sovereign control over the hiring and training of this type of employee.

§5. Training Associations

Training Associations (ASFOs) are bodies set up on the initiative of employer groups at individual sector or multi-industry level within the meaning of Article L. 411-2 of the Labour Code. There are 170 such associations in existence.

The ASFOs as such are not set up on the basis of joint administration in the same sense as bodies such as the Training Insurance Funds. However, some of their activities are delegated by the administration board to control by internal joint committees (Arts. 82-1 to 82-5 of the national multi-industry agreement of 3 July 1991). This rule applies in particular to the allocation of resources for combined training-and-work schemes and resources allocated in accordance with the principle of the collective reciprocity of the ASFOs.

E. Chapter IV. Co-operative consultation within the enterprise

§1. Co-operative consultation and bargaining

Since the Ordinance of 22 February 1945 instituting works councils, vocational training has been within their sphere of competence by virtue both of their management of company welfare facilities (covering apprenticeship and vocational training arrangements in the enterprise) and of their consultative powers. On the subject of their consultative powers, which are by far the more important factor, Article 2(3) of the 1945 Ordinance, as amended by the Law of 18 June 1966, stipulated the following: "The works council must be consulted on general problems relating to training and further vocational training, and to their adaption to employment to take account of technological developments".

This fundamental legislative provision on works councils in regard to vocational training is echoed in the preamble to the national multi-industry agreement on vocational training and further training of 9 July 1970. Its content was specified in more detail by the Law of 16 July 1971 together with the decrees issued for its implementation.

During the 1970s, as continuing training came to assume growing importance in the eyes of both employers and employees, the question of extending the works council's powers in this field was raised on several occasions. For instance, in a report presented to the Economic and Social Council by Monsieur Cheramy it was envisaged that the training plan should be submitted for discussion and approval by the works council: if the council rejected the plan, negotiations would have to be opened between management and the trade unions within the enterprise. An amendment of 9 July 1976 to the 1970 multi-industry agreement settled the issue by unequivocally continuing to confine the works council's powers concerning training to the consultative level. This amendment specified the consultation procedure and its detailed arrangements, and also the nature of the information to be provided to the works council beforehand. The Law of 17 July 1978 on the reform of training leave, trainees' pay and individual promotion followed the same line.

Thus, vocational training remains subject to the dual system of employee representation by both elected workforce bodies and trade unions which is traditional in French law. Neither the Law of 28 October 1982 on institutions of employee representation (Auroux law) nor the Law of 24 February 1984 on the reform of vocational training (Rigout law) abandoned this concept. The unique nature of the employer's ultimate managerial authority is maintained, and the works council's powers in regard to training remain consultative. However, the procedure, content and effects of consultation were again specified in more detail and — a major innovation — a duty to bargain at enterprise level on training was introduced for cases where no such bargaining had taken place at sector level. There was therefore the possibility in some enterprises of complementary intervention by the works councils and the unions in the field of vocational training.

This mechanism for stimulating enterprise-level bargaining on training was abolished by the recent Law of 31 December 1991 (new Art. L. 932-2).

Substantive law on the matter is now characterized by an extremely detailed procedure for information and consultation of the works council, the cornerstone of which is Article L. 933-3 of the Labour Code.

§2. Substantive law

The works council must be consulted "every year" on policy guidelines for vocational training in the enterprise in the light of prospects for the future and changes in employment, investment and technology in the enterprise (Art. L. 933-1). In addition, it gives its opinion every year on the execution of the preceding year's training plan and the draft plan for the coming year. "This consultation shall take place at two special meetings".

The draft plan must take account of policy guidelines on vocational training in the enterprise on which the works council has had to deliberate, the outcome of the negotiations with the trade unions provided for by Article L. 933-2 and, where applicable, the plan for equality at work provided for by Article L. 123-4 of the Code.

"The works council shall, in addition, give its opinion on the conditions for the entry, integration and training of young people in the enterprise, particularly those being absorbed into employment under contracts based on combined training-and-work". This text makes explicit provision for linking between sector-level collective bargaining and works council intervention (Arts. L. 933-2(2) and L. 933-4(2)). It also stipulates that documents supplied to the works council to enable it to exercise its functions should be transmitted to the trade union delegates present in the enterprise.

Also, in cases where the employer draws up a training programme which extends over several years (Article 40(2) of the national multi-industry agreement encourages this) the works council must be consulted on it. The programme must take account, as appropriate, of the objectives and priorities for vocational training specified by the sector-level agreement.

Lastly, it should be noted that in public sector enterprises the works council has more extensive powers in the matter, since the training plan must receive its considered approval. Failing this approval, the plan is submitted for deliberation by the enterprise's board of directors or by the management board following the opinion of the supervisory board.

In this latter case, French law comes closer to the principle of co-determination.

§3. The reality of social dialogue within the enterprise

There is no doubt that, in the great majority of enterprises with more than 50 employees where there is a works council, vocational training is the subject of co-operative consultation between the employer and the workforce's elected representatives, although the degree of its formalization may vary.

The reason why this is so lies in a number of structural factors.

Firstly, the obligation on enterprises to contribute to the financing of training (1.5% of the wage bill) provides a concrete and regular occasion for social dialogue, namely, discussion of the budget: the purposes for which the money should be used, the target groups to be given prioriy, the training-providers to be used, etc. The legislative and regulatory texts expressly indicate the nature of the information which the employer is required to supply to the works council for the purposes of dialogue on training.

The fact that these co-operative procedures are sanctioned by law strengthens their impact accordingly. In addition to the usual penal sanction for the offence of impeding the functioning of the works council, French law imposes a special fiscal sanction in the matter of training: employers who ignore the works council's role are required to pay to the Treasury a penalty representing 50% of the sum they are normally required to contribute towards training.

Secondly, social dialogue within the enterprise is encouraged by the public authorities inasmuch as their own financial contribution is made conditional upon its genuine implementation. This applies, among other things, to the training development commitments which are offered by central government to enterprises or sectors and take the form of a government subsidy to enterprises which operate an active training policy.

Lastly, more and more enterprises are becoming aware of the strategic importance of human resources and training to their continuing business success. Enterprises which practise forms of participatory management are naturally more likely to encourage social dialogue with employee representatives and it frequently leads to enterprise-level agreements on continuing training.

PART III: CONTRACTUAL POLICY ON CONTINUING VOCATIONAL TRAINING IN EIGHT SECTORS

A. CHAPTER I. TYPOLOGY OF SECTOR AND ENTERPRISE POLICIES

§1. The logic of the sector

A number of studies, particularly at CERC (Centre d'Etude des Revenus et des Coûts) and OECD, have used existing data to analyse sectoral patterns of manpower management.

(a) Two authors[1] find that, despite differences in problems and methodology, it is possible to single out predominant sectoral features encompassing a combination of type of activity, predominant approach to manpower management (and hence initial and continuing training) and certain forms of collective bargaining.

They distinguish between several different types of sector. First, "status" sectors are characterized by high wages, large enterprises, high capital investment, a large percentage of skilled manual workers, and a strong state presence either in the form of nationalization or in the form of public markets. They have a strong trade union presence with fairly restrictive collective agreements and a fairly centralized bargaining model. Such sectors include, in particular, coal, electricity, shipbuilding, ores and non-ferrous metals, iron and steel, and oil.

At the opposite end of the spectrum are the "non-status" industries characterized by much lower wages, a predominance of small enterprises, low capital investment and a higher percentage of young workers and female employment. Trade union presence is weak, and several employers' federations frequently co-exist. Collective agreements are not very restrictive and quite often multiple. Such sectors include, in particular, leather, agri-foodstuffs, wood, textiles, etc.

Still others come somewhere between the two models, depending on the particular variables of "status" being considered.

Méhaut and Clément then go on to distinguish between four patterns of adjustment which can be singled out by crossing employment and skills with the role of training.

In the chemical products, pharmaceuticals and electronics industries, the overall trend in employment is positive, with a strong growth in jobs for technicians and engineers. Investment is consistent with this, as is research and development. Initial training plays a strong part in recruitment at the highest levels. Continuing training is used extensively in connection with job moves.

---

[1] Méhaut, P. and Clément, R., *Formation Continue et Négociation Collective en France*. Paris, OECD, December 1989.

In the iron and steel industry, an example of a former status sector now in crisis, training is used in connection with the external re-training of labour, the basic re-skilling of some manual workers, and the formation of new "intermediate categories" through promotion.

The engineering, foundries, metalworking and (to a lesser degree) automobile industries, in a difficult position, are analysed as being "frozen" in their adjustment. They are losing jobs, but their skills structure is not evolving. There is little continuing training, although it could potentially have an important role along with initial training.

The consumer goods sectors such as textiles, wood, leather and footwear employ a very low-skilled workforce, with a high proportion of employees lacking formal qualifications, and a very slowly evolving skills structure.

The volume of continuing training is rarely any higher than the minimum legal requirement.

(b) From another viewpoint, a study by CERC[2] based on data for 1984 analysed company practices on pay and pay supplements. As regards manpower management, although the managerial category was usually treated separately and with more similarities between sectors, the management of non-managerial employees exhibited marked disparities between sectors and also between enterprises within a given sector. Analysis of the sample distinguished four types of manpower management, each cutting across several sectors:

(i)   The category of enterprises with regulated management covers the "big ones" of the automobile industry (car component manufacturers) and enterprises in the basic industrial chemicals and chemical products sector. Most are large. They are characterized by a high proportion of managerial staff, engineers and technicians, a strong preponderance of male workers, a usually small proportion of foreign workers, low mobility and staff turnover and a strong trade union presence. Pay practices are characterized by high manual-worker wages, a relatively substantial level of pay supplements and only small differentials between different categories of employees. Benefits are considerable. There is heavy investment in training, distributed fairly equally between the various occupational categories.

(ii) The category of enterprises with organized flexible management covers the subcontractors to the automobile industry, other enterprises in the chemical products sector and the pharmaceuticals industry (excluding perfume manufacturers), enterprises in the textiles industry and those in wholesale distribution. They have several characteristics in common with the enterprises of the first category; in particular, they are often covered by an identical sectoral agreement (metals, chemicals) or belong to a sector in which the collective agreement forms part of a fairly strong

---

[2] *Documents du Centre d'Etude des Revenus et des Coûts*, No. 87, 4th quarter 1987.

collective bargaining tradition (textiles); and the majority of their manual workers are skilled male workers. However, they differ on a number of points. Their mobility and staff turnover are much higher, the trade union presence is only relatively large and certainly much weaker than in enterprises of the first category, and there is a high rate of dismissals. Pay practices are based on incentives, with much lower wages and pay supplements, much larger differentials between categories and wages closely linked to individual and collective performance, attendance bonuses and more extensive use of forms of profit-related pay. Expenditure on training, although not as high as in enterprises of the first category, still exceeds the statutory minimum and benefits the entire workforce rather than being restricted to managerial staff.

(iii) The category of enterprises with non-organized flexible management covers enterprises in the clothing industry, perfume industry and wholesale distribution. Their industry-wide agreements are not very restrictive. Enterprise-level or plant-level agreements are almost non-existent, and in particular staff turnover and external mobility of labour are very high. Pay practices contain very little incentive element. Manpower management methods make no attempt to foster loyalty or provide motivation. The employee population is generally low-skilled, very often female, easily replaceable and with low unionization. Pay levels are largely determined by the collectively agreed minima. Pay supplements are very small, if they exist at all. Differentials between occupational categories are particularly large. Expenditure on training is limited to the statutory minimum and mainly restricted to managerial staff.

(iv) A fourth and final category covers enterprises in the building and public works sector, in which enterprise characteristics and practices are more homogeneous than within any other sector.

They have a high proportion of male employees, skilled manual workers and foreign workers, and are also characterized by high turnover and mobility of labour between enterprises. The trade union presence is very weak. Wages as such are relatively low, but are increased by pay supplements which are organized and financed within the sector, particularly for discretionary social protection. Expenditure on training is limited to the minimum in these enterprises and almost entirely restricted to the most stable element of the workforce, *i.e.* essentially managerial staff.

It should be mentioned that this sector logic, imposing features which, although flexible, provide a picture of general tendencies for the observer, is not confined to the field of training. Similar effects of the influence on enterprise policy of the particular sector to which the enterprise belongs have been noted, for example, as regards strategic choices in the use of atypical work[3].

---

[3] Amadieu, J. -F. and Rojot, J., *La Gestion de l'Emploi Atypique en Europe: Rapport pour le Commissariat Général au Plan*, Paris 1991, and "La Gestion de l'Emploi Atypique en Europe", *Revue de Gestion des Ressources Humaines*, No. 5/6, January 1992.

§2. The logic of the enterprise

Within these broad tendencies, individual enterprises have considerable room for manoeuvre in choosing their training policies. However, certain constraints apply.

It is clear that training constitutes a major interest at stake in industrial relations at all levels of contact between the social partners, and that collective bargaining is a powerful potential vehicle for its apportionment, even if in many cases bargaining does not operate in practice. Although its intrinsic value is recognized by everyone and on the theoretical level is a matter of broad consensus, its actual implementation encounters clashes of approach.

Apart from the differing positions adopted by the various interested parties, in some cases these positions are not even consistent internally.

(a) For employees, although the training they receive rarely constitutes a "grading" criterion in collective agreements automatically affording them access to a post classified at a precise point in a scale, the fact remains that training is the necessary route to acquiring skills and the driving force behind steps up the career ladder, as well as the opportunity to change direction and/or occupation. In this view of things, it may be felt that access to training should be guaranteed to everyone who wants it. It also constitutes a sometimes heavy investment in a career in terms of time and effort, as a personal commitment, even if the material costs are not borne directly by the beneficiary. Lastly, once acquired it is regarded as something which ought to open up the way to immediate pay increases and improved career prospects.

(b) To employers, training is a tool of company policy which should serve its objectives. Choices, control and decision-making must remain in the hands of the employer, particularly when it is the enterprise which bears the cost. If, however, it is an investment it must be profitable, and the question of the return obtained from the substantial sums spent is often raised. Lastly, the coercive nature of the statutory obligations and the degree of formality surrounding their implementation and possible extension arouses mistrust. The law imposes numerous administrative constraints which, as some see it, impede the flexibility which is needed if proper use is to be made of this training and actually detract from its effectiveness in not giving free rein to those responsible for it,

(c) In considering the possible point of convergence between the respective positions of employees and employers, it may be helpful to turn to analyses centred around the economic theory of human capital[4]. This suggests that, as a matter of degree, the enterprise will become more willing to invest in training for the employee if the training is specific and not transferable to other

---

[4] Becker, G., *Human Capital*, New York, Columbia University Press, 1964, and 2nd edition, Washington, National Bureau of Economic Research, 1975.

enterprises, and less willing if it is of a general nature and easily transferable (unless an undertaking not to leave the enterprise can be obtained from the employee). Conversely, the employee will have a more direct interest in "investing" his personal resources in his own training if it is general, easily transferable and likely to generate a supplementary flow of marginal income whose Net Present Value is greater than the investment made, assuming a subjective internal rate of return which takes account of both the opportunity costs of the investment and its *de facto* likelihood of profitability.

It is unquestionably these lines of reasoning that contain a potential theoretical basis for the principle of co-investment.

(d) Although the various trade union organizations share some basic common options, above and beyond these they have differing priorities which are readily discernible from any record of discussions between union officials or from the trade union press. However, in the first place, their common basis is by no means inconsiderable; in the second place, the five representative organizations may exhibit shades of difference internally, either between organizations in different sectors or between their formal stance and the more diversified practice actually encountered on the ground; and lastly, their formal stances are fairly complex, corresponding to a background of historical development and choices, and it is difficult to summarize them in a few lines in a way that does them justice. It was therefore felt preferable here to present a more generalized analysis illustrating the way in which the stances of the unions, at a fairly decentralized level, may differ from those of the employers, likewise at a generalized and decentralized level since the concept of the employer, ranging as it does from the small craft trades enterprise to the multinational, is similarly altogether too fluid.

In general, the trade unions have been (perhaps even more so in the past than nowadays) anxious to prevent training from essentially becoming, in management policy, one of the means of strengthening employees' commitment to the enterprise and increasing their involvement in the participatory management of human resources. The unions therefore tend firstly to place higher value on training which takes place outside the enterprise and beyond the hierarchical control of management, and secondly to give priority to training which furthers the employee's personal development and autonomy. They feel that continuing training should primarily target activities that give rise to changes in the work situation and enable the employee to improve his control over his job and his working life, to the detriment of types of training which are purely utilitarian from the employer's viewpoint. Lastly, the trade unions are concerned that the definition of the objectives of continuing training given in Article L. 900-1 of the Labour Code, *i.e.* as being "to assist (the) social advancement (of workers) by means of access to the various levels of culture .... and their contribution to cultural, economic and social development", should not be overlooked in comparison with other more immediate and more material objectives. As regards implementation, their priorities are to strengthen the principle of joint administration and to ensure that all categories of employees, including the lowest-skilled and not merely professionally qualified and managerial staff, should benefit from this form of further training.

Above and beyond these general traits, some specific examples indicate particular preoccupations. For example, training may be perceived as a means of protecting skill levels and should make it possible to increase income in the context of the union fight for the right to employment. Also, it should help each individual to gain the opportunity of fulfilling their personal capacity to produce and create. It must be defended against certain ineluctable attempts by employers to put the interests of economic expansion before those of increasing employment and skill levels. Priority is given to public institutions connected with the Ministry of National Education, rather than private training bodies, and to the system of academic qualifications giving automatic recognition of these diplomas in the classification scales of collective agreements.

In another instance, the emphasis may be placed more on autonomy, the personal development which training should permit by making it part of a career path, and hence in particular more on individual training leave and its potential.

In a final example, training may be expected to be more an instrument of employees' general development, particularly outside their work, and so initial training must not be forgotten. Dispensed by public establishments run by the state (in which the social partners are represented), it should improve the position of employees in society, extending beyond the mere collective context within the enterprise.

(e) It is clear that these different ways of thinking make training, beyond the consensus on its usefulness in principle, a field in which bargaining will be lively. A special feature of the French case should be underlined here. In 1971 the legislators made it compulsory for employers to contribute a percentage of the wage bill to employee training (0.8%, subsequently increased to 1.2% and maintained there for a long time, and now increased again since last year), and it is clear that by doing this they supplied a strong catalyst to the discussions surrounding training.

Far from being academic, such discussions became extremely concrete and extremely specific, since a sum of money was thereby created whose minimum amount was no longer a matter for debate but had compulsorily to be made available, at enterprise level, and also had to be spent (on pain of paying an equivalent fiscal contribution).

The eight sector case-studies and individual enterprise case-studies presented below illustrate clearly the issues involved and the variety of the resultant situations.

§3. Contingent nature of the relationship between continuing vocational training and industrial relations

Examples from other countries demonstrate that a wide variety of links are possible between continuing vocational training and industrial relations.

In an analysis which dates from some time ago but is particularly interesting, Maurice, Sellier and Silvestre[5] established that hierarchies, skill levels, structure of employment and division of labour, which of course constitute some of the central elements of an industrial relations system, are all social phenomena which interact and have an internal coherence. This coherence is specific to a given type of society as illustrated by a comparison between France and Germany, and the institutions which express them reflect, themselves, the specific manifestations of social relationships.

Hierarchical relationaships within the enterprise, or the broad features of industrial organization, cannot be understood without preliminary analysis of a specific interconnecting pattern and particular coherence which underlie, in each country, the interaction of three types of social relationships linking individuals to society. One of these is the educational relationship, in both initial training and continuing training. In the case of continuing vocational training, the authors identified two contrasting models of the industrial employment market. The German one is more closed to the rest of the economy but more homogeneous, because the system of continuing training on a combined training-and-work basis allows considerable horizontal mobility between firms and vertical mobility both within and between firms, as a result of the acquisition of skills that are recognized at sector level. The French one is an unstable market, open to non-industrial employment and balkanized into internal markets within firms, as a result of the acquisition of more specific skills based far more, at the time, on recognition by the firm than an independent diploma carrying external recognition.

A more recent study by Catherine Maurice[6] examines the role of training in the management of engineers in electronics companies in France and Japan. She finds that in Japan continuing training is more integrated into company development and strategy than it is in France, despite one or two interesting examples to the contrary. After general basic education, in which they have no part, Japanese companies take complete charge of the employee's integration into employment and manage his career development on the basis of continuing training, which is simultaneously perceived as the vehicle of the company's own development. The company alone decides on the training of its employees, which is seen as an investment. The vocational and technical training system is dominated by the companies themselves, which have their own systems but also make use of external training-providers; its school and university component is totally marginalized. The legal framework is far weaker than in France, and there is an implicit view that vocational training is an integral part of the company's responsibilities. The author notes that training is

---

[5] Maurice, M., Sellier, F. and Silvestre, J. -J., La production de la hiérarchie dans l'enterprise: Recherche d'un effet sociétal, Comparaison France-Allemagne, *Revue Française de Sociologie*, No. XX, 1979, pp. 361-365 and *Politique d'Education et Organisation en France et en Allemagne*, Paris, PUF, 1982.

[6] Maurice, C., *Culture et rationalité dans les formes de Gestion des Ressources Humaines — Le Cas des Ingénieurs de l'Electronique — Une comparaison France-Japon*, Doctoral Thesis, Paris, 1991, Institut d'Etudes Politiques.

given such importance that its organization chart is superimposed on that of the company and of an engineer's career. It is global in nature, encompassing both the employee's integration as a member of the company and the acquisition of knowledge, and is combined with the other aspects of human resource management. Its function in integrating the employee as a member of the company is mainly evidenced in the importance attached to the induction stage and in the fundamental role of on-the-job training. This is one of the major tasks of managers, who are expected to pass on technical knowledge and know-how to their teams while the latter, in turn, communicate any problems and suggestions to them; together, these relationships make it possible to achieve improvements in the production process and product quality. Also, communication and exchange of information are maximized, outside relationships of a hierarchical nature, in a "training organization" which brings about both the sharing of existing knowledge and the production of new knowledge. And training and career are linked.

§4. Bargaining on vocational training in the context of collective bargaining as a whole

Before presenting the field studies, it is important to give some indication of the role of bargaining within the French industrial relations system and, in that context, the relative share of the subject of vocational training in collective bargaining activity as a whole in France. This latter point can be dealt with fairly easily with the aid of figures extracted from the Ministry of Labour's annual assessment of collective bargaining.

(a) First, it should be noted that in the French industrial relations system collective bargaining traditionally plays a relatively secondary role compared with the law. Despite steps taken by the government since 1982 to alter the balance, mainly in the form of a series of successive laws, which have certainly increased the proportion of employees covered by collective agreements, this tendency nevertheless remains strong[7].

At national multi-industry level, many normative and substantive issues which in other countries are regulated directly by collective agreement are regulated by law in France. Furthermore, agreements are closely intermingled with the law. Either an "outline" legal text invites the social partners to complete it, or a law follows and generalizes the content of an agreement. This interaction between the law and bargaining is particularly notable in the field of training.

At sector level, although industry agreements do exist which contain extensive and innovatory provisions, in some instances they merely reproduce the terms of the legislation in force. Supplementary provisions on pay make up the greater part of these agreements. At enterprise level, it should be noted that

---

[7] Delamotte, Y., La loi et la négociation collective en France, *Relations industrielles*, No. 1, 1987.

only 20% of employers are covered by company agreements, the great majority of which are, once again, pay agreements. It should, however, be stressed that some highly innovative agreements do exist at this level, although they are the exception rather than the rule.

(b) Turning, secondly, to the relative share of the subject of vocational training in collective bargaining activity as a whole, it may be said that it ranks only in a secondary, although not negligible, position.

The figures given in the Ministry of Labour's annual assessment show that the predominant topic of collective bargaining is certainly pay. For the period 1988-1991 pay agreements represent between 54.1 and 57.3% of all company agreements, followed by agreements on working hours at between 36.2 and 40.2%. Other bargaining issues lag far behind (1.2 - 5.7% of agreements), and vocational training features as a bargaining issue in only 1.5 - 3.9% of them.

(c) There are, however, a number of considerations which temper this relatively depressing finding. In the first place, much of the social partners' activity in connection with vocational training consists in the administration of fairly complex institutions of variable scope, which is the occasion of multiple contacts and, doubtless, informal negotiations in a more relaxed context.

Furthermore (and this is typically the case with vocational training), other agreements dealing with different but connected areas frequently have major repercussions as regards training. This is so, for example, with a national multi-industry agreement which deals principally with employees on fixed-term and temporary contracts of employment but which covers the conditions of their access to vocational training. The same comment applies equally well, however, to the sector or enterprise level, where agreements on other issues such as classifications, employment or working conditions have a strong impact on, and contain important provisions on, vocational training.

Lastly, there is the existence (non-formalized, but attested by many of the actors encountered) of a very real element of continuing co-operation in many enterprises and industries. Without any form of legally defined written agreement which would be recorded by the Ministry of Labour, the works council at enterprise level and the Joint Committee at sector level meet regularly and constitute forums for contact and exchange where the two sides achieve fruitful progress on numerous issues on an informal basis.

There is no doubt that this illustrates the important role, in a system functioning in a highly centralized environment, of pockets of non-rigidity which are nevertheless administered by the social partners working together.

These latter points are demonstrated by the field study reports which are given in Chapters II and III below. The reports are summaries of the case-studies which were carried out for each sector and each of the two enterprises chosen within each sector, since their length (20-30 pages each) precludes their being presented in full.

These case-studies constitute an initial set of data on collective bargaining on continuing vocational training in France which can be updated as appropriate. They are directed towards singling out innovatory aspects as they were perceived by the actors encountered.

§5. Position of the case-study sectors and enterprises in the context of general statistics on continuing training

Before presenting the essential elements of the case-study findings, however, they need to be placed in context against the general background of statistics on continuing vocational training for all French enterprises and sectors. This can readily be done by quoting figures for enterprises with ten or more employees which are widely known[8] but make it possible to relate what follows to the French situation as a whole.

(a) *General statistics*

The provisional figures for 1990 indicate a contribution rate (proportion of the wage bill spent on continuing training) of 3.20% and hence, as mentioned earlier, an increase over 1989 (2.89%). More than 100,000 enterprises are involved each year. The type of training concerned consists predominantly of training activities forming part of enterprise training plans, which involve more than 3 million employees, as against less than 41,000 instances of individual training leave and more than 206,000 special contracts of employment incorporating combined training-and-work. The proportion of women among all those receiving training has stabilized at 33.6%, and 35.7% of all female employees receive some form of training during the year as against 39.2% of all male employees. This difference decreases among the younger age-groups.

Training effort increases with size of enterprise, the contribution rate ranging from 1.32% for enterprises with 10 - 19 employees to 5% for enterprises with at least 2,000 employees.

The average duration of training is 46 hours when it forms part of a training plan paid for by the enterprise and 52 hours when it is paid for by a Training Insurance Fund (FAF), 878 hours for individual training leave paid for by a Joint Body for the Administration of Individual Training Leave (OPACIF) and 125 hours when this is paid for by an FAF, and, in the case of special contracts of employment incorporating combined training-and-work, 225 hours for employment training contracts of the "contrat d'adaptation" type and 672 hours for the "contrat de qualification" type. The chances of gaining access to training are greater, the higher an employee's occupational category, although this inequality lessens as the size of the enterprise increases. For example, an unskilled or semi-skilled manual worker in an enterprise with 10-19 employees has 2.1% chance of gaining access to training, as against 71.5% for a managerial employee or graduate engineer in an enterprise with 2,000 or more employees.

---

[8] The source of the figures quoted is the *Projet de loi de finances pour 1992* (section on vocational training), Paris, Imprimerie nationale, 1991.

(b) *Relative general position of sectors*

The following table shows, for 1989, the contribution rate of enterprises in different sectors:

Sectors in national accounts		Contribution rate
06	Electricity, gas and water	8.16
04	Coal	5.84
31	Transport	4.96
37	Banking and finance	4.76
36	Insurance	4.38
05	Oil	4.32
07	Iron and steel	4.18
32	Postal services and telecommunications	4.16
15	Electrical engineering	4.02
11	Chemical industry	3.91
17	Shipbuilding and aircraft manufacture	3.32
16	Motor vehicle manufacture	3.31
08	Non-ferrous metals	3.22
12	Pharmaceutical industry	3.14
23	Rubber, plastics	2.85
38	Non-market services	2.81
10	Glass industry	2.50
33	Business services	2.35
01	Agriculture and fishing	2.24
21	Paper and cardboard industries	2.17
03	Other agri-foodstuff industries	2.15
14	Mechanical engineering	2.03
09	Building materials	2.01
35	Letting and leasing of real estate	1.99
26	Wholesale distribution of non-food goods	1.97
02	Meat and milk industries	1.93
28	Retail distribution of non-food goods	1.89
27	Retail distribution of food	1.88
13	Foundries and metalworking	1.87
29	Repair and retailing of motor vehicles	1.84
30	Hotels, restaurants and catering	1.76
22	Printing, newspapers and publishing	1.73
18	Textiles and clothing	1.65
34	Personal services	1.58
25	Wholesale distribution of food	1.55
20	Timber and furniture	1.52
19	Leather and footwear	1.49
24	Building and civil and agricultural engineering	1.38

B. Chapter II. Sector case-studies

§1. Industry

a. Construction

In France, the construction industry encompasses building (new construction, renovation, maintenance) and public works (infrastructures). Although many enterprises, including the largest, have mixed activities, this study is confined to the building sector.

Brief historical background

Collective bargaining activity has been lively at national level both in regard to training and in associated fields affecting it indirectly. Since 1972 a series of national agreements have instituted training policies, priorities, guidelines and bodies at both building sector level and building and public works sector level. In particular, National Joint Committees on Employment (CPNEs) which have powers and responsibilities in regard to training have been set up for both sectors. These Committees, which have held combined meetings, have issued proposals and sometimes reached "agreements" (not to be confused with collective agreements at sector level described below) at such meetings. The most recent dates back to 7 February 1992. All of the social partners have evinced a positive opinion of this agreement, although some did not sign it.

Issues involved

The building industry is essentially made up of craft trade enterprises and small and medium-sized enterprises (in 1990, 76% of enterprises had fewer than 200 employees). Recent technical and commercial changes have led the industry to take a fresh look at its working methods and the skill levels of its workforce. In the face of current developments, issues which it has to tackle include a permanent shortage of skilled labour, the need to upgrade skills, an ageing workforce and a lack of long-term loyalty to the industry, particularly among skilled workers. Training is nowadays regarded as an essential element of employment policy in the industry.

The 1992 agreement concluded within the combined CPNE for the building and public works sectors made this body the central forum for formulating overall sectoral policy on training and employment and guaranteeing its proper implementation.

Revision of the 1985 agreement on continuing vocational training is not on the agenda, owing to the materialization of the agreement of 8 October 1990 on job classifications and the negotiations during 1992 on working hours and more flexible patterns of working time.

The social partners in the industry concluded two agreements on training in 1992, on 20 and 29 October respectively. The agreement of 20 October contains important new provisions on training in small enterprises with fewer than ten employees (stipulation of a minimum financial contribution to continuing vocational training equivalent to 0.22% of the annual wage bill).

The agreement of 29 October represents a response to the request from the partners for "examination of the industry's systems for vocational training and special employment contracts incorporating combined training-and-work with a view to improving the effectiveness of training and the consistency and industry-wide co-ordination of its implementation".

Negotiations on setting up a contractual policy monitoring unit commenced for an agreement covering 1993.

Government intervention

Central government plays an important role. The industry signed a forecasting study contract with the government on 30 October 1990 with the aim of predicting its qualitative and quantitative requirements in terms of labour and skills, and hence its training needs. In addition, a framework agreement was signed with the government on 13 May 1991 for the implementation of training development commitments, including financial assistance for training schemes, in order to encourage modernization and career development.

Follow-up of agreements and joint administration

Firstly, three meetings of the CPNE are planned for 1992. Secondly, several joint bodies have been created. The principle of joint administration forms part of a corporatist tradition with which the industry has always been associated. The Continuing Training Group for building and public works combined (GFC), set up in 1972, is a Training Insurance Fund (FAF) and Approved Funds-pooling Body (OMA) for enterprises with 10 or more employees, and also an Approved Joint Body for individual training leave (OPACIF) for the industry. It is administered by a joint council and bureau, with permanent staffing, and is relayed via 25 regional training associations (which are also joint bodies). In total, it comprises 700 employer and employee representatives and 200 permanent staff. There are 23,367 member enterprises.

The Training Insurance Fund for craftsman employees in the building industry is for small-scale craft trades enterprises with fewer than 10 employees and has 150,000 members. Set up in 1989, it collects contributions through the intermediary of the National Pension Fund for building workers and redistributes them through bodies operated by the employers' organizations in the industry. There is a problem in that only one FAF may in principle be approved for each industry: the GFC is already one such, and this FAF for craftsman employees in the building industry has also requested approval.

In addition, the Central Co-ordinating Committee on Apprenticeship for the building and public works sector, set up in 1942, receives financing in the form of an employer's contribution of 0.30% of the wage bill. This committee is more specifically concerned with initial training and is also an OMA for enterprises with fewer than 10 employees.

Innovatory elements

The industry feels that it has made considerable efforts in regard to young people. It has invested heavily in training for tutors and apprenticeship masters for the purposes of increasing the intake of young employees and fostering the transmission of knowledge at all levels, particularly in enterprises with fewer than 10 employees. It has a policy of decentralized response to regional needs.

On 2 February 1993 the industry signed an agreement with the Ministry of Labour on training for young employees whose jobs are at risk. This agreement uses the funds normally reserved for combined training-and-work formulas. Its purpose is to enable almost 5,000 young employees aged under 26 whose jobs are at risk to undergo training without their contracts of employment being terminated. It gives priority to the acquisition of level V skills.

An agreement of 8 October 1990 contains innovatory elements such as the establishment of a training/classification/skills link, the recognition of diplomas not recognized by the Ministry of National Education, the promotion of combined training-and-work formulas, the validation of internal periods of training within the enterprise, and the acknowledgement and recognition of professional experience as a qualification alongside formal diplomas.

European perspectives

The employers' associations belong to the European Industrial Federation for the Construction Industry, which maintains a dialogue with the European Federation of Building and Woodworkers and wishes to be recognized by the Commission as official negotiating party for the building and public works sector.

b. Textiles

The textiles industry is separate from the clothing industry, with its own collective agreement.

Brief historical background

Sector-level agreements and other agreements on vocational training have been concluded between the social partners since 1974 in the case of the latter, and in general regularly since 1984. The most recent dates back to January 1990. Negotiations on job classifications and more flexible patterns of working time are in progress.

Issues involved

The industry is essentially made up of small and medium-sized enterprises (93% of enterprises have fewer than 200 employees). Their numbers have declined by 25% since 1985. Of the total, 45% are located in two regions of France, namely, Nord and Rhône-Alpes. In addition, the impact of robotics and automation is bringing about a technological revolution and increased productivity. The traditional manual occupations are disappearing, whereas a growth in demand is expected for technical managerial staff and multi-skilled manual workers.

In terms of substantive provisions, the agreements on training add only modestly to the statutory and national multi-industry agreement provisions, with the possible exception of the means accorded to trade union delegates and works council members.

Government intervention

This has been evidenced by the conclusion in 1985, after consultation of the trade unions, of a framework agreement between the industry and central government on the implementation of a training development commitment, which was renewed in 1988. Its objective was to facilitate training in new technologies. A new framework agreement on training development was signed to run from 1992. It aims to "prolong and augment" the positive effects of the 1985 and 1988 agreements. This agreement is to a large extent based on conclusions drawn from the forecasting study contract.

The forecasting study contract was signed in a similar fashion for the purpose of defining trends in the industry's training needs, taking a time horizon of 1995. Its conclusions serve as a basis for the policy outlines defined above.

Follow-up of agreements and joint administration

A tripartite follow-up group analyses activities in the area defined by the framework agreement on the implementation of the training development commitment.

A joint national committee on training, as distinct from the Joint National Committee on Employment (CPNE), was set up under the 1990 agreement so that training issues, on which there is more consensus, could be dealt with separately from issues relating to employment, which are more problematical. It meets at least once a year. The CPNE met only rarely, although contacts took place on an informal basis. This new committee is intended as a forum of negotiation, but also deliberation, on technical matters such as the career skills ladder ("parcours qualifiant") for manual workers.

There is no national joint body responsible for collecting or administering sums originating from employers' contribution to the financing of vocational training.

At regional level a multitude of structures may exist, differing widely in number and method of functioning in individual regions.

Innovatory elements

The new committee mentioned above, set up with the intention of singling out the potential consensus on training, is one innovatory element. For the employers (Union des Industries Textiles), the deliberations on a career skills ladder for manual workers, based on an analysis of different occupations and skills, constitutes another. For the trade unions, the problems of validation of the skills acquired and their incorporation in the classification scale remain open.

For the observer, it is interesting to note the adoption in certain individual regions of the joint administration which is not present at national level. A similar point of interest is a regional agreement (Roubaix-Tourcoing-Valleé du Lys) on leave for education in economic, social and union affairs which contains favourable provisions.

European perspectives

None reported, but there is a noticeable preoccupation with the need to adapt to international competition.

c. Metals

The metals sector is extremely diversified, with coverage ranging from the production of ores and non-ferrous metals to shipbuilding and aircraft manufacture.

Brief historical background

Although collective bargaining on the objectives of vocational training takes place at national level, the implementation of agreements is decentralized. The 1985 agreement on the objectives and means of vocationl training underwent re-negotiation, leading to the agreement of 31 March 1993. The new provisions added to the 1985 agreement by this 1993 text chiefly concern apprenticeship and initial technical training, and special contracts of employment incorporating combined training-and-work. A 1983 agreement created "metals" sections in the Funds for the Administration of Individual Training Leave (FONGECIFs). A 1987 agreement on general employment problems, amended in 1990 and 1991, also contains important developments regarding training.

Issues involved

The metals sector is the largest in French industry, with 2 million employees. Of this total workforce, 23% are located in the Paris region and 13% in Rhône-Alpes. The remainder is scattered with less than 5% in a given region. Bargaining powers on employees' rights are centralized in the employers' organization for the sector as a whole. The employers' organizations for the various subsectors have exclusively economic and technical powers. It is a highly diversified sector, ranging from the small enterprise to the large group: it contains large enterprises and only 9% small-scale craft trade enterprises, 45% with fewer than 200 employees and 35% with 500 or more. The majority of employment is manual work. Its future prospects indicate a reduction of the workforce, particularly unskilled workers.

Government intervention

A forecasting study contract was concluded between the Federation of Metal and Mining Industries (UIMM) and central government, giving rise to studies on the state of continuing vocational training.

Follow-up of agreements and joint administration

The National Joint Committee on Employment (CPNE) meets twice a year to examine the employment and training situation in the sector at national level. Its tasks include prospective qualitative analysis of jobs, the use of employment training contracts incorporating combined training-and-work (particularly "contrats de qualification" accompanied by certification), providing employees with information, and establishing training priorities.

There are regional Committees (CPTEs) which perform the CPNE's role at regional level with varying degrees of activity.

There is no joint administration body at national level, and only two Training Insurance Funds (FAFs) resulting from agreements in Sarthe and the Ardennes, However, there are Training Associations (ASFOs) in all of the regions, set up by groups of employers to promote, guide and provide training activities at enterprise level. Their management board is joint, but its role in the administration of funds originating from the statutory financing of training by enterprises is limited to a small proportion of the money.

Innovatory elements

The key element is unquestionably the procedure for the validation of skills by the CPNE on a joint basis.

Its principle is the result of deliberations on the form of employment training contract referred to as the "contrat de qualification". It has four interesting special features. A skill implies the definition of a vocational goal expressed in terms of "being capable of " and not completion of a pre-established training programme, which is therefore attainable via diverse training routes from different levels of ability. It also implies the definition of an instrument of measurement which may be a final examination but also some other quite different method. Its identification and definition are the responsibility of the industry concerned, but it must be validated by the CPNE for the metals sector or, more accurately, by the joint technical working party which the latter has set up internally. Lastly, the identification and definition of the demand for skills are carried out on the authority of the regional industry associations, but the pertinence of the demand and its definition is evaluated, at national level, by the joint technical working party. Testing is conducted at regional level, whereas the award of certificates is carried out, again, at national level under the control of the joint technical working party. It should be noted that the trade union organizations are not wholly uncritical of this procedure, even though they have endorsed its broad outlines.

European perspectives

These exist in connection with contacts between European organizations and partners. The employers' organization has already entered into discussions on the reciprocal recognition of qualifications.

d. Chemical industry

For the purposes of the study, this sector covers the basic chemical industry (heavy and fine) and allied activities, excluding the pharmaceutical industry.

Brief historical background

Numerous agreements deal indirectly with training or have an impact on it, such as the employment agreements of 1969,1970,1987,1990 and 1991, the 1990 agreement on technological change and the 1992 agreement on the improvement of working conditions and health and safety. Bargaining on training is not regarded as an area in its own right by the social partners, but as an instrument of adaptation for enterprises and employees and as an investment. Contractual policy in the industry is comprehensive and looks for "quality" of bargaining. The employers' policy in regard to training is one of active participation by the social partners.

The 1985 agreement on the objectives and means of vocational training underwent re-negotiation which led to an agreement of 28 April 1993. The French Democratic Confederation of Labour (CFDT) and the French Christian Workers' Confederation (CFTC) have not signed this new agreement and stress the inadequacy of the means which it grants at enterprise level to guarantee its proper application.

Issues involved

The industry is concentrated: enterprises with over 200 employees represent 17% of the total number and those with over 500 represent 7%, but they respectively employ 80 and 62% of employees in the industry. The number has decreased by 17% since 1980.

The job structure reveals a much higher than average proportion of qualified engineers, managerial staff and technicians, whose numbers are growing, whereas the numbers of manual workers (particularly the unskilled) and white-collar workers are declining. The skill level of the manual workers is also higher than average. The problem at present is a mismatch between enterprises' needs and the supply on the labour market, not in terms of what is deemed an adequate level of education but in terms of a supply of knowledge of the "industrial" type which is sought both for qualified engineers and for plant operators.

Rapid technological changes have taken place and are still in progress.

Assessment of the 1985 agreement reveals a qualitative improvement in training, plus the fact that the social partners (and almost half of all enterprises) think that it has helped them.

Government intervention

In 1990 a forecasting study contract with central government was signed which includes the participation of enterprise experts in five committees in order to take stock of current technical and organizational developments and their implications for the management of employment and the adaptation of training. Follow-up action is taking place in a joint context. Some of the conclusions were taken into account in the re-negotiation of the agreement on vocational training.

Follow-up of agreements and joint administration

The National Joint Committee on Employment (CNPE), created in 1969, meets five times a year. Its responsibilties in regard to continuing training include examining needs and issuing opinions, ensuring follow-up of the agreement, participating in the study of public and private means of training and co-operating with public authorities and bodies, examining the re-training of employees belonging to categories which are on the decline, defining training priorities, compiling lists of courses of interest to the industry and skills attainable under employment training contracts incorporating combined training-and-work, and ensuring follow-up of forecasting studies on trends in jobs and training.

It has served for a long time as a forum for dialogue, at least as far as training and skills are concerned.

There is no Training Insurance Fund (FAF) at national level, and only one at regional level, in Nord-Pas-de-Calais. The other regions are organized around Training Associations (ASFOs) with a joint management board, as in the case of the metals sector.

In addition to certification by the CNPE of skills that can be acquired under employment training contracts, there is certification in the form of vocational accreditations awarded by the vocational training committee of the employers' association on completion of a modular training fulfilling specified criteria.

Innovatory elements

In this sector too, the key element is the establishment of a joint certification procedure as described above.

Employers alert their regional industrial association to any demands for skills which are non-existent on the market and necessary to the functioning of the enterprises. A formal request for approval is then drawn up, including in particular the definition of the skill required, expressed in terms of abilities. Following approval by the CPNE, the introduction of this strand of training leads to a better matching of vocational skills to the proposed jobs.

This system for the validation of skills learned in the context of a special employment training contract meets the following needs:

– achieving maximum flexibility to allow a rapid response to contract requirements; it therefore comprises a decentralized procedure based on the

regional industrial associations, which draw up the request for approval by the CPNE (which has exclusive authority to award certification);
- keeping as close as possible to the real needs of the job; consequently, it excludes direct approval of ongoing training activities so that the starting-point is not existing supply but demand;
- defining the vocational abilities to be attained, and the criteria for their validation, in order to occupy a particular job; this definition of the vocational goals of the skill needed is expressed in terms of "being capable of", which gives the procedure more flexibility and adaptability to the varied needs of enterprises while responding to the wish to make forms of certification transferable.

European perspectives

The social partners in the sector, mindful of the social (as well as economic) consequences and implications of the construction of Europe, believe that it is necessary to add another dimension to national bargaining: a new, autonomous contractual route in the shape of Europe-wide bargaining. All of the partners are already uniting at European level and reflecting on the conception of a different form of bargaining, but also on the development of a new manifestation of the principle of joint decision-making.

§2. Services

a. Banking

The sector is a highly diversified one. Banking law classifies credit institutions into several categories: banks, mutual-benefit or co-operative banks, savings-banks or provident associations, municipal credit establishments, finance companies, and specialized financial institutions. Each category is subject to detailed regulation in its particular field of operation. Two types of establishment exist side by side: general-purpose establishments, such as the leading commercial banks, and special-purpose establishments which cater for a particular type of clientèle or operate within a particular range of activities.

Brief historical background

In the field of continuing vocational training the banking sector pre-empted all the legislation on training, since the first centre for training in banking was set up in 1932. The sector therefore did not wait for the legislation of 1971 and is not geared to the same approach. Traditionally, hiring itself is accompanied by a number of vocational training provisions and then, throughout their career, employees have the opportunity of access to courses and to instruction organized by the sector.

A national agreement on the objectives and means of vocational training for employees was concluded in 1985. This was re-negotiated, and has been supplemented by an agreement dated 12 February 1993. The latter text includes new provisions mainly relating to apprenticeship (negotiations on this issue are on the agenda). It specifies the conditions whereby training clauses can be invoked.

There was also a 1989 agreement on reform of the courses taught by one of the sectoral training bodies, the Technical Institute of Banking (ITB). Lastly, an agreement of 1991 reformed the Vocational Certificate for Banking.

Issues involved

The French banking system encompasses 425,000 employees and contains both world-scale establishments and modestly sized establishments of widely varying legal status.

The growth experienced in the 1970s led to the hiring of large numbers of employees at a fairly low level, which is now creating an age pyramid problem. The sector has witnessed and is still witnessing a period of accelerated change, and in particular the multiplication of increasingly sophisticated products and services, the amalgamation of establishments and the increased use of computerized techniques for increasingly complex applications. The educational level of recruited employees is therefore particularly high; the minimum is now baccalauréat level for most jobs. The qualifications structure is 18.8% managerial staff, 60.7% supervisory/technical and 20.5% white-collar clerical workers. Owing to the recruitment level, the decline in clerical workers in favour of graduates will continue. At present, the employers' organization sees the total workforce as decreasing by 2 or 2.5% per year, which can be covered by natural wastage. In 1990 some 11,000 individuals were hired, which means that a reduction of the workforce is manageable.

For the next three years, the banks envisage some 12,000-13,000 recruitments per year.

In the case of the banks, the rate of financial contribution to vocational training in 1989 was 5.09%, as against the average of 2.9%.

Three training bodies provide the sector's internal continuing training:

– the Banking Vocational Training Centre (CFPB), which provides pre-banking instruction on a combined training-and-work basis for young people entering the profession, training leading to the Certificate of Vocational Competence(CAP) or Vocational Certificate (BP), plus advanced training and seminars, and runs the Technical Institute of Banking (ITB, higher education in three years);
– the Centre for Advanced Banking Studies (CESB), which provides complementary training for senior managerial staff;
– the Technical Markets Institute, which provides intensive specialized training.

Re-negotiation of the collective agreement for banks is in progress, with provision on training and human resource planning.

Government itervention

The sector follows the official regulations closely, but its tradition of strong internal training means that they do not concern it directly. Central government intervention is therefore minimal.

Follow-up of agreements and joint administration

The Joint Committee on Employment (CPE) holds meetings on training which deal with topics such as the reform of all banking vocational training courses, preparations for the introduction of new courses, and the signing of joint sector-level agreements on the conditions of access for candidates to these forms of training.

The agreements on training within the sector which were mentioned earlier are further examples of joint decision-making on the matter.

Innovatory provisions

The agreement of 21 June 1991 (on the Vocational Certificate of Banking) introduces innovations as regards access to training. An assessment test prior to the commencement of training is used as a basis for defining a recommended path of training. In conjunction with this, the diploma is broken down into cumulative units and employees who have already attained the required standard in a subject may be granted exemption from an examination. The course has been designed entirely for adults possessing employment experience, with appropriate forms of teaching and a conception of the trainee as an active participant in their own training.

Co-investment is involved for the students of the Technical Institute of Banking, who attend half of their courses outside working hours.

The validation of skills acquired through training is provided for under the collective agreement for banks, which automatically recognizes the Vocational Certificate of Banking both in terms of classification and in terms of a specified number of points which are directly reflected in the employee's pay.

As regards access to training, a tutoring system is provided for young people hired under an employment training contract, whose numbers are increasing. More generally, fairly wide use is made of contracts incorporating combined training-and-work in the sector, since they account for more then 10% of new recruits.

European perspectives

Banking has been international since its beginnings, and the sector participates in several European associations which have training goals. As far as the major banking institutions are concerned, they all have linking networks and training centres which provide meeting-points for managerial staff from different countries.

b. Insurance

The sector contains companies which engage in both personal insurance and property insurance; contrary to practice in some countries, they are not separate.

Brief historical background

Agreements concluded in 1969 provided for the formation of a National Joint Committee on Employment (CPNE) for clerical workers, and then managerial staff, with responsibilities for training. A national agreement on the objectives and means of vocational training for employees and the introduction of forms of combined training-and-work for young people was signed in 1985. This was followed by an agreement in 1989 on the employment of disabled persons.

After lengthy discussions, negotiations concerning the national collective agreement for the insurance sector led to an agreement dated 27 May 1992. This text contains numerous provisions relating to vocational training, including the creation of a bonus for experience (which in future will replace the length-of-service bonus) and the introduction of an individual training "account".

Issues involved

The sector has a workforce of 216,850 people highly concentrated in a small number of companies, with 10% of companies accounting for more than 70% of employment.

The number of "employees" in the strict sense (121,300), after a period of considerable growth in the 1970s, has remained fairly stable since 1983 and it is unlikely to undergo any major variation in the next few years. In addition to these employees, insurance agents, brokers and experts bring the number in the total workforce to 216,500.

The insurance sector is faced with changes linked to new technologies (computerized methods in particular), the expansion of its market and an opening-up to Europe, and new developments in its regulation. Some traditional jobs, mostly corresponding to low skill levels, are declining or disappearing. Balanced against this, an increase in the number of managerial staff and supervisors is predicted, together with a general upgrading of skills due, in the main, to the ongoing training of existing employees and the predominance of young people with baccalauréat +2 qualifications among new employees hired.

The employer's contribution to continuing training is increasingly seen as an investment. On average, insurance companies spend 4% of their wage bill on further training. The sector's own training establishments organize continuing training in the following forms: under the Association for Insurance Training (AEA), training leading to the Advanced Technician Certificate (BTS) in insurance; under the National College of Insurance (ENAss), a management training course and a commercial course; and under the ADAP (insurance training centre), short training courses.

Government intervention

In the case of training, excluding the regulation of the sector activity, there appears to be very little apart from the original tripartite nature of its management as described below.

Follow-up of agreements and joint management

In addition to its "employment" activities, the CPNE has subcommittees which are responsible for monitoring diplomas and their content and matters relating to the reform of vocational training.

The ADAP (insurance training centre) offers companies short training courses not leading to any formal diploma, collects the apprenticeship tax, a large proportion of which is used to finance the other training bodies, and administers forms of combined training-and-work for the sector. In this respect it acts as an Approved Funds-pooling Body (OMA) for the insurance sector. Its board of directors is made up of employers, as is its general meeting, but the training board is of joint composition.

Issues relating to continuing training are discussed and combined training- and -work is "co-managed".

The National College of Insurance, which was founded in 1946 (ENAs and CHEA), is managed on a tripartite basis and financed by a parafiscal charge (from the start) and also, nowadays, partly by the employer's contribution for continuing training and partly by the apprenticeship tax.

The Association for Insurance Training (AEA), which is intended for training at non-higher education level, is under joint administration. It caters for the majority of employees: Certificate of Vocational Competence (CAP), Vocational Certificate (BP) and Advanced Technician Certificate (BTS).

Innovatory elements

Sectoral provisions intended to assist the access of young employees to certain forms of training: paid time off for young employees following certain courses, with registration costs borne by the employer.

The agreement on the employment of disabled persons, which sets up a joint administration body responsible for employment and training problems.

Without question, the introduction of an individual training "account" is the sector's most original feature. This account consists of a "credit" of 400 hours which can be used over an employee's entire career and is intended to enable them to compensate or alleviate any difficulties of adaptation they encounter, on their own initiative. It is confined to holders of the baccalauréat who have completed at least three years' service with the same employer.

European perspectives

Insurance is one of the sectors chosen by the Commission in Brussels as a vehicle for the concrete realization of European social dialogue. Following concerted consultation between the Commission, the European trade union organizations and insurance companies within the European Insurance Committee, a decision was made in July 1990 to open up sectoral dialogue. This dialogue is to relate to issues specific to the sector as chosen by the partners which do not touch on multi-industry or technical matters. Training was selected as a primary issue, the initial aim being to assess the systems for training in insurance which exist in the various EC Member States.

International collaboration is also active within the sector.

c. Retail distribution

Within the retail trade, the general distribution of food was chosen as a clearly identified sector.

Brief historical background

Bargaining on vocational training has included an agreement of 1971 which set up a National Joint Committee on Employment (CPNE), followed by a 1985 agreement on continuing vocational training and an agreement in the same year on managerial staff. These were supplemented in 1988 by a framework agreement on technological change and an agreement on terms and conditions applicable to employment training contracts.

Here again, the provisions form part of a more widely ranging contractual system of sector-level collective agreements. It should also be noted that there is, in addition, an informal bargaining aspect: the trade unions were closely involved in the agreements negotiated between the employers' organization and central government which are analysed below.

Issues involved

The sector is undergoing rapid change, meaning that the market share of establishments with large sales areas has increased steadily, to the detriment of other forms of outlet and in particular small independent retailers, in a context of increasingly keen competition, mainly in terms of prices, which has led to accelerated restructuring and concentration.

The number of employees, which has shown a low growth rate over the past ten years, is around 370,000.

The workforce is young, predominantly female, with a high turnover, low skills level and preponderance of fixed-term contracts or part-time work. In approximate figures, there are more than 80% white-collar workers, 6% managerial staff and 10% technicians and supervisory staff, 40% of the latter having been promoted internally. The proportion of non-graduates is very large. In terms of skill levels, there is a very wide gap, without any intermediate posts, between white-collar workers and supervisory and managerial staff.

The rate of financial contribution to training is below the national average (1.79% of the wage bill as against 2.10% in 1988) in enterprises of all size categories, although it is on the increase, particularly in large enterprises. Training is concentrated on managerial and supervisory staff.

Government intervention

This has been notable in the retail distribution sector. A forecasting study contract was signed in 1988, followed by framework agreements on the development of apprenticeship and a training development commitment (EDDF) in 1990 and 1991 and agreements with the region or Ministry of National Education.

Follow-up of agreements and joint administration

An aspect to be noted is the involvement of the trade unions in the negotiation of contracts and framework agreements between employers and central government and the union presence in the bodies formed under agreements with central government, such as the technical working party on vocational training provided for by the agreement with the Ministry of National Education. In addition, the government aid resulting from the EDDF agreement of 1991 is to be administered jointly.

The CPNE's role includes providing information, carrying out studies and supplying enterprises with directly useable tools such as certification models or training programmes.

The sector has no joint administration structure, other than that in the case of apprenticeship an employers' organization has been approved as the tax-collecting body and that co-operative enterprises (which are a minority element) have a Training Insurance Fund (FAF). There is, however, one Training Association (ASFO), which performs a function different from the customary activities of such bodies, particularly as regards the study and development of training.

Innovatory mechanisms

Examples include co-operation with the Ministry of National Education for the purposes of recruiting and consulting young people, and investment in the training of apprenticeship masters and tutors for forms of combined training-and-work. The ASFO's specialization in the study and development of training is notable. Lastly, the social partners made special mention of the manner in which negotiations on job classifications were conducted, in stages and with shared analysis in the course of the process.

European perspectives

These are not really taken into account as far as training is concerned. On the other hand, in terms of business strategy there is very strong awareness of interaction with other countries.

d. Hotels and Restaurants

The sector is identified as comprising hotels, cafés and restaurants. It covers all enterprises of this type, with the exception of catering contractors, canteens and hosting centers. It forms part of the tourism business, and constitutes its key element.

Brief historical background

The hotels and catering sector is one of the few not to have a national collective agreement. There are, however, regional agreements (Ile-de-France and Côte d'Azur for tourist hotels) and national agreements, to which the official extension procedure is not applied and which are confined to particular activities in the sector: hotel chains, restaurant groups, fast-food outlets. Employer representation is very fragmented in numerous organizations, and the large number of small enterprises and seasonal workers makes trade union activity difficult. The use of employment training contracts is the only area in which a debate has opened up and in which there are national agreements to which the official extension procedure has been applied. One of these, in 1974, set up a Training Insurance Fund for the hotel industry (FAFIH). The next, in 1982, set up the National Joint Committee on Employment (CPNE). In 1985 there was an agreement on the absorption of young people into employment, which was amended in 1987.

Vocational training was the subject of an amendment added to the 1985 agreement on 27 October 1992.

Issues involved

The sector is very dispersed, and has a majority of sole proprietorships: almost 50% of enterprises have no employees, 90% have fewer than 6 employees and only 4% have 10 or more employees. Of the total of 585,000 employees, 50% work in the hotel chains. Hotels represent only one sixth of the total number of enterprises.

The sector is expanding, in terms of both number of hotels and number of rooms. Within the hotel industry, the chains are increasing in number while the independents are on the decline. It has the unusual feature of combining a labour-intensive activity with, at the same time, heavy entry investment.

The workforce increased by 6.4% between 1983 and 1989 and the sector has created more than 30,000 jobs a year over the past few years, although the majority involve short-term contracts. In 1989, 23.5% of employees were aged under 25 (as against the average of 14%); labour turnover is very high and the industry has difficulty in recruiting, with a particular shortage of skilled workers, owing to the long working hours, fairly low pay and tempory nature of many jobs.

More than 50% of employees have no diploma, but this figure was 93% in 1963. Traditionally, diplomas have only minor importance as a criterion for hiring new employees and internal promotion prevails.

Training exhibits special characteristics, and is dictated by the labour market. Initial training, the enterprise and continuing training are seen as three indissociable facets for which it is imperative that they should be co-ordinated by the industry itself. The proportion of the wage bill devoted to training is below the national average (in 1989, 1.76% as against 2.89%), but the trend is upward and the larger part of the training provided goes to the unskilled.

Training is the only area in which contractual policy exists at all, yet even here it is limited (apart from the creation of joint institutions) to the restatement of legal obligations.

Government intervention

This is minimal. There is no forecasting study contract; the industry's request for one incorporated co-financing by the FAFIH, and was refused.

Follow-up of agreements and joint administration

The absence of such a contract handicaps the work of the CPNE. It has, nevertheless, initiated several studies on the employment of managerial staff, the accreditation of the Technician Certificate for the hotel industry, etc. The CPNE is decentralized into Regional Joint Committees on Employment (CPREs).

The FAFIH, which is the only Training Insurance Fund in the sector, collects compulsory contributions of variable amounts from enterprises, assessed on their statutory contribution to continuing training. It administers training leave, and thus has the status of a Joint Body for the Administration of Individual Training Leave (OPACIF) and collects the contributions for this purpose, and is an Approved Funds-pooling Body (OMA) for the purposes of forms of combined training-and-work. It is the FAFIH, and not the enterprise, which signs agreements with the training body.

The FAFIH is decentralized, like the CPNE, and the two maintain close links.

Innovatory mechanisms

In two regions, a link-up between the National Employment Agency, the CPREs and the employers' organizations in order to identify and train job-seekers who possess the necessary abilities.

The attempt by the FAFIH to regulate the training market, by approving and authorizing bodies responsible for training.

A programme for the integration of young people, and the employment and training of seasonal workers.

The idea of extending the benefit of training to non-employees, since the majority of enterprises are sole proprietorships and the heads of enterprises are, by definition, non-employees.

European perspectives

These are minimal.

C. CHAPTER III. ENTERPRISE CASE-STUDIES

§1. Industry

a. Construction

Enterprise 1

Brief historical background

This is a family-type enterprise which nowadays constitutes a group consisting of several subsidiaries, with multiple activities and 1,250 employees. It has opened up 20% of its capital to employee share ownership. The management view is that it is the people who make up the enterprise who ensure its performance and guarantee its future. Among the enterprise's key values, training is regarded as the instrument and preferred means of realizing people's potential and integrating new arrivals through knowledge of building industry skills and the enterprise.

In 1975, the commitment to training was either limited to what constituted a legal obligation, or it was used as a form of bonus, or it was purely and simply absent from personnel management. Today, the enterprise devotes almost 4% of its wage bill to training (7% if the pay of young people on employment training contracts is included). It has engaged in several operations in partnership with the National Employment Agency or the CFI, with success. It possesses its own training body. In 1991 a proposal for a training development commitment was submitted to central government.

Issues involved

The quality of forms of combined training-and-work is being improved through the creation within the enterprise of genuine routes for the transmission of knowledge.

The scheme for individualized career development through training is linked to the enterprise's wish to give preference to internal promotion. Its origin is directly associated with conclusions drawn from analysis of the age pyramid, which is too high. It poses the question of links between training and job classification, etc.

These arrangements are in line with one of the principles defined at sector level on training policy which is recognized in the new job classification of the collective agreement of 8 October 1990, and the role of tutor was already included in the sectoral agreement of 20 February 1985 on the objectives and means of vocational training.

Results of bargaining

None. The works council was consulted and endorsed the scheme. There is no training committee. There are no trade union delegates.

Innovations

The importance attached to the proper introduction and functioning of the tutoring system and the scheme for individualized career development through training, as well as the partnership with the National Employment Agency. The very existence of such arrangements in an enterprise of this size is exceptional in itself.

Enterprise 2

Brief historical background

This is a building and public works enterprise, with vertically diversified activities and approximately 1,280 employees.

The enterprise's management has developed a policy on upgrading occupations in the building industry, reflected in a policy of *rapprochement* with the Ministry of National Education, and a policy on the integration of employees which takes the form of sponsorship and a series of vocational training courses starting on initial entry and following on throughout an employee's career.

In 1990 the percentage of the wage bill spent on continuing training, having increased by 0.5% annually since 1988, was 4.5%.

Issues involved

Integrating young people, whom the enterprise has opted to recruit at a high level (CAP - Certificate of Vocational Competence), and retaining them within the enterprise, in the face of a high labour turnover in an industry which, rightly or wrongly, has a rather unattractive image.

Strengthening professionalism by providing means for the transmission of know-how at all levels and deriving full value from the existing stock of experience.

Forms of training which lead to diplomas take place within the sectoral context and are financed by the Training Insurance Fund (FAF) for the building and public works sector.

Results of bargaining

None. The enterprise has a works council, workforce delegates and trade union delegates.

Innovations

The range of successive courses accompanying an employee's career, and the partnership with the Ministry of National Education.

b. Textiles

Enterprise 1

Brief historical background

The managers attempted to relate personnel management as closely as possible to orders actually received, over a maximum of one year in advance. The enterprise, which is a subcontractor to the automobile industry, suffered a crisis in 1985 which forced it to diversify and to carry out redundancies.

Issues involved

The manual workforce has to undergo re-skilling and profound changes in mental attitude and working methods in order to become more multi-skilled in the face of the demands imposed by diversification.

Results of bargaining

None as regards training. The works council was consulted but has had little invovlement. However, in 1986, 1987 and 1988 agreements were negotiated with the General Confederation of Labour (CGT), the only union with a presence in the enterprise, on the reduction of working hours, adjustable working hours (annualization, for example), and 18 redundancies

Innovations

Co-operation with the GRETA at département level (Ministry of National Education) in preparing a form of combined training-and-work to CAP (Certificate of Vocational Competence) level for young people. This introduced the enterprise to internal training using tutors. Preparations for the operation, which entailed giving an overall view of the enterprise, gave rise to meetings involving the workforce in a total quality approach.

Enterprise 2

Brief historical background

The enterprise has been operating for many years in a favourable context. It belongs to a group specializing in the development and manufacture of wovens for industrial use. Internal training is a recent introduction. Training activity forms part of a long-term approach, and every instance of training is intended to lead to a new job definition involving more autonomy and responsibility, giving rise to a higher grading and hence an increase in pay. The overall approach is aimed at making employees more responsible and multi-skilled in a move towards enhanced productivity and total quality.

Issues involved

Competition is forcing the enterprise to improve its performance, and its internationalization is imposing increased requirements for quality and conformity with European standards. In addition, the enterprise is experiencing recruitment difficulties at senior technician level, given the posts and levels of pay offered and some degree of rejection by qualified young people. It is therefore a matter of increasing the general skills level.

Results of bargaining

None. There is no trade union representative in the enterprise. However, consultation and even informal and personal "negotiations" take place within the works council, which through its training committee is closely involved in, among other things, the enterprise's training plan.

A major internal training programme has just been introduced by local enterprises and the département GRETA (Ministry of National Education), in which this enterprise is participating at
Certificate of Vocational Competence (CAP) level. The technical segment, which takes place within the enterprise, is staffed by tutors, namely, manual workers belonging to the enterprise who endorse this training.

With GRETA assistance, the enterprise is establishing an occupational and teaching reference system. It has already been granted aid from the Ministry of Labour for the development of training in the textiles industry. An application has been submitted for aid under a training or adaptation agreement from the National Employment Fund.

Innovations

The intermeshing of training, skills and quality.
The close involvement of the works council.
A form of co-investment which belies its name since general upgrading training is outside working hours.

c. Metals

Enterprise 1

Brief historical background

The case-study relates to then existing policy, because in August 1992 the enterprise was to be taken over by the Schneider group. The enterprise makes electrical and electronic equipment and has a workforce of 31,000 employees at group level, with 8,000 of these in the parent company. A company agreement has been in existence since 1972, and is re-negotiated at regular intervals or supplemented by amendments and special agreements. The enterprise set up an internal training centre which was approved by the AFPA. An operation launched in 1985 was aimed at adapting 1,000 employees whose jobs were at risk to 1,000 new posts which would become necessary. Such was its success that it even resulted in a modification of training policy. This led to a framework agreement on training which was signed in 1990.

Issues involved

Skills are changing in the metals sector. The enterprise has a tradition of negotiating with the social partners which was strengthened through the meetings on its 1,000=1,000 operation. The outcome left the workforce highly motivated by training. However, although lengthy training is a good solution for young workers it is not so for low-skilled employees aged over 40.

The 1990 framework agreement

This restated and formalized, at the trade unions' request, all of the practices which were present in the enterprise. It was signed by all of them except the General Confederation of Labour (CGT).

The role of the works council's training committee is very important. In particular, apart from providing information and analysing training plans, it keeps a check on their satisfactory progress and has quarterly meetings with those responsible for vocational training.

Innovations

In addition to the close association of the social partners mentioned earlier, the following may be noted: a new compartmentalization of training into the institutional (FMB, *i.e.* basic modular training), the specific (meeting a specific need) and the individual (career management for an individual employee); FMB itself, which is intended to raise the general level of employees who have not gone beyond secondary level; the principle of co-investment applied to 40% of the time spent on FMB; the voluntarist principle of the 1,000=1,000 operation; and the scheme, as part of training to upgrade professional skills, under which training which imparts skills but does not lead to a diploma is linked directly to career and personnel management (followed by skipping a grade in the job classification, after observation in the work situation itself).

Enterprise 2

Issues involved

Following the serious crisis suffered by the enterprise in 1984, with a deficit of 12,000 million francs, the main issue was the enterprise's survival by virtue of profound changes, made not only to its industrial relations policy but also to the technical organization of its production system.

Confronted with new economic conditions and competition, it had to adapt and change. This involved more autonomy for employees, greater responsibility and a higher skills level.

The principle underlying the agreement was: "Tomorrow, the company will essentially be made up of the men and women who constitute it today".

Results of bargaining: "Contract to Live"

The main issues and topics broached were:

– human resource planning, with the creation of an occupations monitoring unit;

– the introduction of an induction path for new young employees, backed up by personal interviews and possibly supplemented by a potentiality assessment;

– without question, the most important element of this agreement was the part devoted to professional competence and training. The scheme for the skills upgrading of operators, based on voluntarism and targeting the unskilled manufacturing workforce, was complemented by a system of individual further training intended for all employees and implemented outside working hours;

– lastly, the company wanted these forms of training to be recognized by a national or regional validation system, and wanted the actual organization of work in the enterprise to enable these new skills to be put into use. Thus, it wished to develop a new type of work organization founded on basic units which were small in size and made up of multi-skilled members performing enriched tasks.

Innovations

Access to the acquisition of skills: the scheme for the skills upgrading of operators is the most innovatory element of the system, since it targets all of the unskilled operators and affords them access to a higher skills level, without the level thus attained being recognized in the job classificaion scale.

Validation of skills acquired through training: it introduced an individual upgraded skills record card intended to capitalize the training received, but the "contract" makes no mention of recognition in the company agreement of new skills acquired through training, even though it undertakes to consider it.

Co-investment: long before the Law of 31 December 1991 providing for the possibility of co-investment in training, it had already introduced this arrangement, particularly for training leading to a diploma or new skills. It takes the form of 13 types of training outside working hours for which there is no question of the training costs being paid by the employee. This idea of shared effort is present throughout the "contract" in order to give employees more responsibility and make them active agents in their own career.

Similarly, it pre-empted the legislative provisions of 1991 with its introduction of a potentiality assessment for all employees who request it when there is a radical change in their work.

Training is placed at the centre of the enterprise's human resource policy. The "contract" creates the link between human resource planning, career management, skills management, organization of acquisition of skills, and training.

This "contract" was the first of its kind to have been signed by five of the six representative unions at enterprise level. It opens up the way for other discussions and new agreements. It reflects the implementation of a new type of labour relations within the enterprise.

d. Chemical industry

Enterprise 1

Brief historical background

The enterprise employs just under 5,550 people in health, allied pharmaceutical and chemical activities. There are plans for a restructuring, involving job cuts but no compulsory redundancies. There is a history of negotiating with the social partners. Agreements were concluded in 1989 and 1990 on a profit-sharing scheme, pay and end-of-career leave. There is no agreement on training.

Issues involved

In 1991 the percentage of the wage bill allocated to training amounted to 4.66%, a drop from 5.36% in 1990 and continuing on from 4.95% and 2.94% in 1989 and 1988 respectively. The explanation for these fluctuations lies in the introduction in 1989 of the collection of data on training needs and the launching of various forms of training in 1990. As this increased effort shows, the group regards training as an essential tool of human resource management. The workforce contains a high proportion of female employees at the white-collar worker, technician and supervisor levels. An effort is made by management to foster employee communications. The range of tools used in human resource management is in the process of being enlarged (mapping of jobs and generalized use of the appraisal interview).

Results of bargaining

None as regards training, but they exist elsewhere. Training involves four actors: line management, the workforce itself, and the central and local training services. There is, however, co-operative consultation in the context of think tanks with employees and one instance of a discussion group on modernization with the unions in an establishment. Similarly, management is involving the social partners in its examination of the adaptation of employees following the reorganization of chemical activities. Lastly, the central works council has an active training committee.

Innovations

General management training for high-potential managerial staff, plus the planned introduction of a right to training and assessment, a policy privileging internal promotion and action in favour of equal opportunities for men and women.

Enterprise 2

Brief historical background

The group occupies important positions in packaging, aluminium, industrial components and allied activities. It wishes to maintain or improve these positions. Labour policy is viewed by management as a major component of its strategy. This is reflected in the encouragement of general deliberations at plant level on two topics: changes in the organization of work and the forward planning of skills management. Numerous applications are in progress.

Issues involved

Training policy forms part of the two axes mentioned above, as one of the keys to their success in developing not only knowledge but also ability. The subsidiaries and individual plants are encouraged to devise skill training programmes based on combined training-and-work and the validation of skills acquired through such training. Framework agreements have been signed with the Ministry of National Education by the largest companies in the group. The administration of managerial personnel, and the associated training policy, is centralized at group level.

In 1991 the percentage of the wage bill devoted to training amounted to 3.8%.

Results of bargaining

Above and beyond the proper functioning of employee representative bodies, it is the group's intention to promote contractual policy as much as possible in all areas of its labour policy. In 1990, 52 agreements were signed in the companies belonging to the group. At group level, there is a group works council, a European Information Committee and a joint negotiating body. Two agreements were signed in 1990 and 1991: one on the right to organize and the duties and careers of trade union representatives, and the other on changes in work organization and the forward planning of skills management.

Innovations

These are implicit in what has already been mentioned: the group is moving from a logic of planning (jobs) to a logic of building up a capacity to respond to uncertainty by involving employees in changes to the organization of work and in the management of their skills; and this is in a contractual framework negotiated with the social partners. Lastly, the European Information Committee, a discussion and information body providing dialogue between the group's general management and the representatives of employees in EC countries on strategic options, will certainly find a fruitful area in training.

§2. Services

a. Banking

Enterprise 1

Brief historical background

This is one of the large nationalized banks and employs 42,000 people in France. A series of agreements have been concluded between management and the social partners on a multitude of subjects such as pay, part-time work and participation, including an agreement on training. In 1988 the workforce decreased by 1%, as it had every year since 1975, mainly as a result of incentives for voluntary redundancy presented to the works council. The use of vocational training is a traditional practice in the bank.

Issues involved

The enterprise devotes 6.65% of its wage bill to training. In addition to the programmed reduction of the workforce that has been in process since 1975, it is conscious that the changing trend in jobs is towards a considerable decrease in the proportion of clerical workers. An intensive career guidance and re-training operation will be needed.

Results of bargaining

The 1989 agreement on training was signed by all of the unions except for the General Confederation of Labour (CGT). It is regarded as a tool of human resource planning. Training forms part of the enterprise's overall strategy and is viewed as an essential investment.

A typology of jobs is in progress. Arrangements for training are decided annually, on the basis of available information. There are 90 training plans, one for each establishment, which conform to the general policy guidelines defined at group level after consultation of the central works council.

Innovatory provisions

The introduction of an assessment procedure in order to validate the training received.

The personal commitment exhibited by those who receive training. Although it does not constitute co-investment, the idea is to demand involvement from beneficiaries.

Training activities relating to career changes, with formalized successive phases of training and tutoring. Note should also be taken of the trend away from training leading to a diploma towards training which imparts new skills without leading to a formal diploma.

b. Insurance

Enterprise 1

Brief historical background

The enterprise is at present in a favourable economic situation, increasing its market share in a market which is itself buoyant. The workforce is growing. This is making it possible to arrange for the number of agents to increase while reducing the number of clerical workers rendered surplus by computerization and the quest for productivity gains, without needing to introduce a redundancy programme.

The bargaining culture, and especially bargaining on vocational training, is already long-established. Furthermore, training plans were submitted to the works council for approval, not merely for consultation. Numerous company agreements have been concluded on a great many topics.

Issues involved

The age pyramid is too stongly concentrated on the 35-45 age group. The workforce contains a relatively small proportion of graduates, particularly among certain categories. The average length of service is high. Lastly, certain jobs are disappearing while other new ones are appearing, and many are changing. An analysis of employment has been carried out and a social dialogue initiated.

Results of bargaining

The "trajectory" agreement on employment-training-mobility was signed in 1990. It attempts to identify employment issues upstream and declares the principle that economic considerations and labour relations considerations cannot be dissociated. It organizes human resource planning based on co-operative consultation with line management, the social partners (a joint follow-up committee has been set up) and the workforce. It aims to develop training adapted to employment forecasts and to smooth the way for internal mobility.

Innovations

The "new occupations" plan based on specimen jobs and skills management.

A re-training contract which will offer priority training to employees occupying jobs which are expected to become "vulnerable" in the future, accompanied by a guaranteed transfer to a job corresponding to the new skill acquired (with a probationary period).

c. Retail distribution

Enterprise 1

Brief historical background

Founded in 1961, this enterprise is one of the leading hypermarket companies in France. In 1991 it achieved a turnover of 45.8 billion francs in its 45 stores distributed throughout four regions, employing 27,600 people. It belongs to a group (60 billion francs turnover, 45,000 employees) which has also developed specialist sales outlets and restaurant outlets and has established itself in Spain, Italy and the USA.

Since the outset, the company has evolved around what is seen as a highly specific business philosophy: customer satisfaction and economic profitability necessarily go hand in hand with human and social development founded on shared knowledge (training and information), shared power (initiative and responsibility) and shared benefit (sharing of the fruits of labour).

Vocational training has long been seen as a strategic axis of development. The target set by the founding chairman is to achieve 10% of working time spent on training and information per employee per year. In 1991 the enterprise devoted 3.8% of its wage bill to training, which is far above the average for the sector. An ambitious training development programme extending over several years (1991-1995) provides for a substantial increase in the training budget every year. In order to speed up its training effort, the enterprise has also applied for government aid under the training development commitment (EDDF) signed by the sector.

With the active participation of management, the enterprise has established:

– at national level: the Institute of Training in Excellence;
– at regional level: four training centres;
– at the level of each store: a department of basic training in excellence.

Issues involved

In the face of mounting competition and growing demands from consumers, it is seen as vital for the company to upgrade the professional competence and status of its workforce by means of both horizontal training courses (hypermarket employment as an occupation) enabling them to adapt to changes in the enterprise and the economy, and vertical training courses (product-related occupations) specific to each department enabling them to perform their tasks and adapt to changing trends.

In addition, training is a means of providing motivation and opening up promotion opportunities, and a channel for disseminating the enterprise's ethic, culture and values.

Results of bargaining

Apart from the central works council, within each store there is an establishment-level works council, a training committee, workforce delegates and trade union delegates.

There is a company agreement on human resource planning ("Individual career development of white-collar workers") dated 1 October 1990. There is no specific agreement on training. The central works council was consulted on, and unanimously approved, the training proposals which the enterprise submitted under the EDDF.

Innovations

Training is entirely centred around personal career development. The training courses mentioned (horizontal and vertical) have been national and compulsory since 1 April 1991. They involve all categories of employees (in 1992: 2,945 white-collar workers/manual workers, 114 supervisors, 45 managerial employees). Assessment interviews, whose findings are processed by computerized analysis, make it possible to keep track of of the trend in employees' professional competence and status.

Training has become an operational requirement; even employees on fixed-term contracts receive training.

The close involvement of line management gives internal impetus to all training activities down to the level of individual section heads.

The tutoring system used in forms of combined training-and-work has been transferred to internal training (especially for young section heads): the tutor's role combines that of providing training and monitoring the skills acquired.

Enterprise 2

Brief historical background

In 1991 the group achieved a turnover of 30 thousand million francs and employed 24,000 people. It comprises 50 hypermarkets, 220 supermarkets, 74 cafeterias, 28 shopping centres and 598 sports shops. As at 31 December 1991, the hypermarket company was employing 5,378 people. It should be noted that the group has recently been taken over by another retailing group (June 1992).

The training department has been in existence for only three years. It comes under the group's chairman. In 1991 the percentage of the wage bill devoted to training was 2.17%, which was in line with the average for the sector (1.89% in 1989) but below the national average (2.89% in 1989, 3.14% in 1990).

Issues involved

One of the enterprise's priorities is training for newly hired employees. This is because, as in most retailing companies in the large sales area category, labour turnover is high: in 1991, 1,502 employees had been working for the company for less than 3 years, and almost half of the workforce (2,547 employees) had been with it for less than 6 years.

The significance of internal promotion motivates the enterprise to develop pre-promotion training.

Results of bargaining

Non-existent. In the words of the head of training: "The social partners have no more of a role to play in training than they do in marketing, for example, because training is not an employee benefit but an investment". This clearly ignores the powers and responsibilities of the works council in economic matters (of which training forms a part).

Innovations

In this very decentralized training system, the role of line management is extremely important. Decisions on training are taken in the board of directors with the six regional directors who are the real decision-makers and who are therefore directly involved in the implementation of the schemes which are approved. The line managers (store manager, department heads, section heads) play a part in the successive delegation of training. All department heads have completed a five-day training course for training-providers to help them in carrying out their function.

In addition, one of the training department's tasks is to devise relatively straightforward teaching aids which are easy for non-experts to use. The enterprise pays considerable attention to multi-media training in this connection.

d. Hotels and restaurants

Enterprise 1

Brief historical background

The company belongs to a group which in 1991 had a turnover of 3.32 thousand million francs, chiefly in light industry (42.7%), the mass-market hotel industry (21%) and the luxury hotel industry (34%). With 372 hotels and 32,700 rooms, the group is the second-largest French hotel group. Its management is essentially of the family type.

The company being studied, which manages the luxury hotel segment of the business, had a turnover of 1,128 billion francs, representing a fall of 5.6%. This poor result was attributed to the economic situation, since the company actually achieved significant gains in productivity, mainly by reducing the number of employees and withdrawing certain acquired rights. Thus, in the establishment in which the study was carried out the workforce decreased from 822 permanent employees in 1991 to 640 in 1992. It should be noted that a department of human resource management has just been created in this hotel; prior to that no training policy existed. The training budget corresponds to the statutory minimum.

Issues involved

The workforce has a level of initial training below baccalauréat (70%), and more than 40% of employees are foreign workers. In the face of current technological and social changes, the enterprise finds itself obliged to get training "under way" in an establishment where no such tradition exists. There is no contact with the sectoral associations.

Results of bargaining

None. Unionization is mainly high among the employees with the lowest level of education, who have the least access to training and demand it least. Consequently, training is not a subject for claims or of any real interest to them (mostly members of the General Confederation of Labour, *i.e.* CGT).

The unions attend the statutory meetings on training.

Innovations

In order to motivate employees to be trained, the enterprise has instituted an active system of communication: via line managers, via individual question-naires and via opportunities for interdepartmental contact aimed at breaking down internal divisions. As a result, in addition to technical courses a system of training is developing which is informal (not costed) but relatively effective.

Enterprise 2

Brief historical background

The enterprise belongs to an international group (turnover 16 thousand million francs and 54,181 employees) which has just been taken over by the leading French hotel group (turnover 22.4 thousand million francs and 82,402 employees). The latter's beginnings date back to 1967, but in its present form the group has existed since 1983 and encompasses more than 45 company names.

From the outset, the group has viewed training as a strategic priority, enabling it to disseminate its management philosophy and company culture and to strengthen its internal coherence. This is why it established, in 1985, a company university which catered for more than 14,000 trainees in 1991.

The enterprise studied, which has 400 employees, devoted 1.6% of its wage bill to training in 1991. The group to which it now belongs is giving it strong encouragement to expand its efforts in this area.

Issues involved

Training is used to increase the professional competence of the workforce both on the technical level and in terms of customer relations and team management. It is also used as a way of transmitting the values and ethic of the group and to integrate newly acquired enterprises, as is the case here.

Results of bargaining

None within in the enterprise. The works council and training committee are consulted as laid down by law.

At group level the social partners are difficult to mobilize on the issue. At a more global level, the group was intending to set up a European social concertation body in 1992.

Innovations

A very close linking of employment and training (integration and development of employees) and the introduction, to this end, of training plans extending over several years.

The considerable cultural value attributed to training.

Development of the international dimension through management courses.

GENERAL CONCLUSIONS

The aims of this analysis of the relationship between collective bargaining and vocational training in France were to establish a factual account for the purposes of Europe-wide comparison and to identify those elements judged to be innovatory by the actors questioned. The present conclusions deal only with this latter point, on which the following comments may be made:

A. Developments and innovations affecting the continuing training system

1. In the case of initial training, internal changes taking place within the French education system are likely to strengthen the hitherto limited influence of the social partners. We are referring here, of course, not to basic and general education but to technical education and the apprenticeship system. The newly evinced awareness of the education authorities to the importance of strong links with the production system, the influence of decentralization (Law of 1983-84) and the recent reform of the apprenticeship system all signal this development trend.

The social partners have themselves strongly affirmed their strategic will in this area (national multi-industry agreement of 1991). This constitutes the first innovation that should be emphasized: "The signatories have drawn attention to the special responsibility of the social partners with respect to basic technical and vocational training, especially at individual sector level, in the definition of skills and, consequently, of guidelines and priorities on diplomas and validation methods. They have also specified conditions for the entry and follow-up of young people in apprenticeship or training courses in enterprises".

2. In contrast to this, the continuing vocational training system, as it has developed from 1970 onwards in its current form, is by its very nature anchored in the industrial relations system, as the education system is not. The continuing training, re-training and skills qualification of employees fall within the natural sphere of competence of the social partners and collective bargaining. The innovatory elements relate to the importance that has now been assumed by combined training-and-work (*formation en alternance*), as a subsystem of continuing vocational training, for the purpose of providing young people aged 16-25 with career guidance and adapted or new skills under special contracts of employments combining employment and training. The administration and financing of this system, and the recognition of skills acquired through training and experience, are very largely the responsibility of the social partners and implemented through collective bargaining and joint administration procedures.

The second innovation to be noted, which concerns the continuing training system as a whole, is the social partners' intention, as strongly expressed in the national multi-industry agreement of 3 July 1991, to make this system and its internal coherence their own. And, by the same token, their intention to attempt to reduce government control in this area.

3. From the outset, the French industrial relations system and collective bargaining law have envisaged the treatment of continuing training as a bargaining issue. Both the general law of collective bargaining and the law dealing specifically with continuing training testify to this: continuing training is regarded as a social guarantee, it is one of the compulsory provisions for collective agreements eligible for being made generally applicable under the official extension procedure and negotiations relating to vocational skills must mention formal diplomas. Here, the innovatory elements are of three kinds:

(a) The statutory obligation imposed on the social partners in 1984 to engage in negotiations on continuing vocational training every five years has had the progressive effect, following an initial phase of purely formal response, of increasing the awareness of sector-level negotiators to the importance of this issue. As the case-studies show, the "results of bargaining" at sector level are certainly of interest.

(b) There is a definite correlation between the quality of the results of sector-level bargaining and the existence of "forecasting study contracts", that is, methodological and financial support from the public authorities for sectors which decided to undertake analyses of employment and skills before entering into negotiations.

(c) In its traditional form, joint action by the social partners at sector level constitutes collective bargaining which produces norms or guidelines and sets up institutions. In the particular field in question here there are, in addition, two long-term elements, namely, the Joint Committees on Employment, and other joint-administration bodies dealing specifically with particular aspects of the continuing training system: Training Insurance Funds (FAFs), and Approved Funds Pooling Bodies (OMAs) dealing with individual training leave or combined training-and-work. The growing prominence of the principle of joint administration, with recognition of its legitimacy and effectiveness for the administration of social guarantees, is a striking feature of the French industrial relations system.

4. The unique nature of the French continuing training system lies in its source of financing. There is a statutory contribution of 1.5% of the wage bill for enterprises with 10 or more employees and 0.15% for enterprises with fewer than 10 employees. (On average, enterprises actually spend 3.60% of their wage bill on continuing training.)

Its impact on the relationship built up between the industrial relations system and continuing training has been decisive.

This statutory provision has had an indisputable structuring effect on the French continuing vocational training system and lends it coherence, in terms of both the specific allocation of money and the amount made available. The social partners' involvement in steering policy in continuing vocational training in France rests largely on this financing mechanism.

1. Structuring effects of the financing mechanism as such

Any enterprise which does not organize training activities itself, entrust them to external bodies or discharge part of its obligation in contributing to the appropriate joint bodies (leave for combined training-and-work), is required to pay its vocational training contribution direct to the Treasury. Needlless to say, few enterprises opt for direct payment.

This financing mechanism has had the following structuring effects within the individual enterprise:

– greater awareness on the part of employers of the value, and indeed the strategic importance, of training. The obligation to draw up an annual training plan and approve an annual training budget has played some part in teaching them this awareness;
– an upgrading of the professional competence and status of the enterprise's training department (in enterprises with more than 500 employees) or setting-up of inter-enterprise training services by groups of employers;
– in enterprises with more than 50 employees, the establishment of social dialogue with the works council as routine practice, not only as a statutory obligation but also for the practical purposes of budget allocation. Although the debate is often formal, the fact that meetings take place on a regular basis allows time for more conflict-prone issues to be dealt with as objectively as possible whenever they arise;
– similarly, a structuring effect on the nature of the training provided, and indeed the definition of continuing training. This is because, whereas in the broad sense any human activity may include an element of "training" for the individual experiencing it, the law has necessarily used a more restrictive definition. Its definition of the training activities which fall within the category of those to be financed by the enterprise represents the most functional definition of continuing vocational training ever used in France;
– lastly, a structuring effect of the method of financing individual training leave and combined training-and-work. Owing to the use of the "mutualization" technique, the relatively small sums compulsorily paid by each enterprise into an approved joint fund enable the social partners to pursue autonomous training policies. Thus, paid educational leave has come to be used as a vehicle for long-term training undertaken to earn promotion at work, and combined training-and-work is taking shape as a modernized form of the traditional apprenticeship system.

2. Structuring effects of the volume of this financing

The potential volume of financing made available annually is approximately 40 billion francs, *i.e.* matching the 40 billion francs spent by the government on its budget for similar purposes. This amount is large enough to have repercussions on the system and on the strategies of the actors, mainly those of enterprises but also those of the social partners, training-providers and central government. The magnitude of the financing available has therefore made continuing training a strategic issue in France. And it is precisely because of this that the the social partners are able to intervene in it in a consistent manner, using their own special know-how: defining policies, negotiating the rules of the game, assessing the outcome of policies implemented, shifting the rules of the game to respond to new priorities or increase the effectiveness of enterprise training activities, etc.

The stability of this volume of financing, with its annual availability, has also prompted the development of training provision of a new kind, not shaped by the academic system but geared first and foremost to demand on the labour market, with which the social partners are directly familiar.

This has led to the increased specialization of providers of continuing training and the gradual emergence of a new profession, with its own set of regulations on materials and methods and its own association. This is benefiting the coherence of the system as a whole.

Although the basis of the obligation imposed on enterprises is fiscal in nature, in terms of practical implementation it remains so only very marginally, in the form of the possibility of government control. The government does not act as a tax collector; the situation is, rather, that the magnitude of the resources available prompts the government to attempt to steer the course of events by issuing laws and regulations that have been "negotiated" beforehand with the social partners or seeking out financial partnerships.

B. Developments and innovations within the system

Within the French continuing training system, analysis of the results of bargaining (Ministry of Labour's annual assessment of collective bargaining) and scrutiny of the sector and enterprises case-studies conducted for the purposes of this study reveal the following major trends:

1. Innovations in sector-level bargaining

(a) The combined training-and-work formula represents the major area of innovation at sector level. The following aspects may be noted: provision for taking account of professional experience possessed by the employee which has not been acquired through formal training; the emergence of the function of tutor as the modern-day form of the apprenticeship master; and, above all, new arrangements for the organization and certification of the acquisition of vocational skills on the responsibility of the social partners themselves. Thus, a function traditionally performed by the state is being partially transferred to the social partners.

(b) Employee access to training is now also defined in terms of "qualitative" conditions as well as the conditions governing entitlement imposed by training leave or the enterprise plan: better knowledge of the job and other occupations within the sector, or the organization of "paths" leading to certain skills.

(c) The search for ways of involving employees more closely in their work and training should also be mentioned (e.g. banking). Here, it takes the form of "co-investment" of time, with the employee accepting that part of his training should take place outside working hours.

2. Innovations in enterprise agreements

(d) The detailed aspects of the implementation of combined training-and-work formulas are found in enterprise-level agreements: the role of tutors, ways of taking informal professional experience into account, and the validation and recognition of the skills acquired through training.

(e) The subject of co-investment features more frequently at this level than in sector-level agreements (although still only on a modest scale), more particularly in the form of co-investment of time (metal).

(f) The policies of modernization and upgrading of human resource management which were pursued by numerous enterprises in the mid-1980s, particularly large public enterprises, gave rise to some highly innovatory enterprise agreements.

Here, training features as a tool serving the changes undertaken. It is seldom the subject of bargaining when it applies to management, but becomes a bargaining issue when associated with the introduction of modern skills management policies or changes in the organization of work.

The "Contract to Live" agreement is a prime example of the integrated approach: training and skills management. It deals more particularly with access to the acquisition of skills for unskilled workers, skills assessment, the validation of skills acquired through training, co-investment, etc. Two other enterprises adopt a similar approach: in banking and insurance.

(g) The chemical agreement establishes an original and innovatory link between training and planned changes in the organization of work. The traditional logic (individual-training-skills) is replaced by a new logic: organization-training-skills. A new link is thus created between training leading to skills and a form of work organization which uses them.

Modification of the contract of employment for the employees concerned is provided for.

*   *   *

A deliberate search for innovations in the results of bargaining such as that reported here, based on the case-study findings, probably over-emphasizes the positive side of the picture. The reality may well be less positive in many sectors and enterprises. The fact remains, however, that in cases where collective bargaining on continuing training takes place it does appear to constitute a vehicle of innovation and dynamism. And in cases where it does not take place, the results of bargaining elsewhere undoubtedly help to shape the attitudes and behaviour of the social actors and enterprise human resource managers.

SELECTED BIBLIOGRAPHY

J. -F. AMADIEU and J. ROJOT, La Gestion de l'Emploi Atypique en Europe, Report for the Commissariat Général au Plan, Paris 1991, and La Gestion de l'Emploi Atypique en Europe, *Revue de Gestion des Ressources Humaines*, No. 5/6, January 1992.

CENTRE INFFO, Les accords de branche, dossier spécial, *Actualité de la formation permanente*, No. 79, Nov.-Dec. 1985.

R. CLEMENT and Ph. MEHAUT, Formation continue et négociation collective en France, Report for OECD, Nancy GREE, 1989.

A. d'IRIBARNE and A. LEMAITRE, La place des partenaires sociaux dans la formation professionnelle en France, Research report for CEDEFOP, LEST., January 1987.

P. GUILLOUX and A. JUNTER-LOISEAU, Contribution de la négociation collective de branche à l'amélioration des relations entre formation et l'emploi, *Actualité de la formation permanente*, No. 47, July-August 1980.

P. GUILLOUX, Premier bilan de la négociation de branche sur les objectifs et les moyens de la formation professionnelle, *Droit Social*, Feb. 1986, pp.151-157.

P. GUILLOUX, Négociation collective et adaptation professionnelle des salariés aux évolutions de l'emploi, *Droit Social*, No. 11 November 1990, pp. 818-832.

P. GUILLOUX and J. M. LUTTRINGER, Validation et reconnaissance des acquis de formation par les branches professionelles et les entreprises, approche juridique, Centre d'Etudes et de Recherches sur le Droit Social, Université de Paris-X, Nanterre, MADIF 1992.

P. GUILLOUX, Les commissions paritaires de l'emploi et la formation professionelle continue, *Actualité de la formation permanente*, No. 58, May-June 1982 and No. 59, July-August 1982.

A. JOBERT and M. TALLARD, Le rôle du diplôme dans la construction des grilles de classification professionelle, *Bilan annuel de la négociation collective 1990, Les dossiers*, No. 4.

J. M. LUTTRINGER, Le droit de la formation continue, Dalloz, 1986.

J. M. LUTTRINGER, L'obligation de négocier la formation continue dans l'entreprise, *Droit Social*, Feb. 1986, pp. 145-150.

J. M. LUTTRINGER, L'accord national interprofessionnel du 3 juillet 1991 relatif à la formation et au perfectionnement professionel, *Droit Social*, No. 11 November 1991, pp. 800-806.

Ph. MEHAUT, Syndicats patronat et formation: les fonds d'assurance-formation des salariés, Presses Universitaires de Nancy, 1982.

J.F. NALLET, Les fonds d'assurance-formation des salariés, fonctionnement et politique, Centre Inffo, Paris, 1981.

J.F. NALLET, Les comités d'entreprise et la formation continue, Centre Inffo, Paris, 1978.

M. TALLARD and N. BESUCO, Formation - classifications - emploi, analyse des accords d'entreprise, CEREQ-DRT study, *Bilan annuel de la négociation collective 1991, Dossier* No. 1.